C000173963

How to Implement Effective Relaxation Techniques

Learn How To Reduce Stress And Anxiety In
Just 7 Days With Proven Relaxation Techniques

Michael Robertson

© Copyright 2020 - All rights reserved.

The content contained within this book may not be reproduced, duplicated or transmitted without direct written permission from the author or the publisher.

Under no circumstances will any blame or legal responsibility be held against the publisher, or author, for any damages, reparation, or monetary loss due to the information contained within this book, either directly or indirectly.

Legal Notice:

This book is copyright protected. It is only for personal use. You cannot amend, distribute, sell, use, quote or paraphrase any part, or the content within this book, without the consent of the author or publisher.

Disclaimer Notice:

Please note the information contained within this document is for educational and entertainment purposes only. All effort has been executed to present accurate, up to date, reliable, complete information. No warranties of any kind are declared or implied. Readers acknowledge that the author is not engaged in the rendering of legal, financial, medical or professional advice. The content within this book has been derived from various sources. Please consult a licensed professional before attempting any techniques outlined in this book.

By reading this document, the reader agrees that under no circumstances is the author responsible for any losses, direct or indirect, that are incurred as a result of the use of the information contained within this document, including, but not limited to, errors, omissions, or inaccuracies.

Table of Contents

Introduction

"Set peace of mind as your highest goal, and organize your life around it." Brian Tracy

It's normal to experience stress. We all go through stressful situations at some point in our lives. These situations range from minor nuisances like traffic jams to more serious issues like losing your job or a loved one. When faced with these stressful situations, our bodies are flooded with emotions, our anxiety levels increase, our hearts beat faster and our muscles tense. Well, this is how the body responds to stress and anxiety. In fact, it's normal for the body to enter into a "fight or flight"(stress) response. It's a deep-rooted response that helps us to survive through threatening situations.

The truth is that we cannot avoid the diverse sources of stress that we're constantly exposed to. Nonetheless, we can choose healthier ways of responding to these stressors. One effective way of doing this is through "relaxation response." For most of us, relaxation means zoning out in front of our television sets or flopping on the couch at the end of a tiresome day. In reality, this does little to help us overcome stress and anxiety. Activating your body's natural stress response, on the contrary, puts your body in a state of deep rest. It is in this state that you can achieve peace of mind and relieve yourself from stress and anxious thoughts that are wearing you out.

Practicing relaxation techniques helps to quieten your mind. Your body and mind are brought to balance. There are different types of relaxation techniques that you can turn to. Some of these include deep breathing, yoga, rhythmic exercise, tai chi, meditation and so on. It's worth noting there is no single relaxation method that works for everyone, as we all have varying relaxation points. The way your body enters into a deep state of rest is different from how another individual would relax. This means that the right relaxation technique for you is one that resonates with you. Your ideal technique should be the one that can help your mind relax and evoke the relaxation response you direly need. More importantly, it should fit your lifestyle.

With the plethora of relaxation techniques available out there, you need to try these methods until you find the right one that suits you. It's then that you will continue practicing these relaxation techniques to ensure that you overcome everyday stress and anxiety. Ultimately, this will help boost your mood and energy, improve your sleep and enhance your overall health and wellbeing.

When stress gets the best of you, even the people who seem to be the strongest can find it daunting to find their Zen again. Worst, the emotional burden of stress builds up overtime. Unfortunately, this affects your life in every way. It robs you the joy of being in the present moment to enjoy life as it unfolds itself. It prevents you from experiencing growth through challenges. This happens because you will have a pessimistic outlook towards life.

Fortunately, you can learn to silence the outside world through the relaxation techniques that will be discussed and effectively described in this guide. Maybe you've been struggling to calm your mind and that it appears overwhelming because stress and anxiety seems to build up. The more you think about the challenges you might be going through, the more stressed and anxious you get. So, if you're going through a rocky relationship, a financial predicament, loss of a job, or that you're simply overthinking about your future, all these can greatly contribute to anxiety disorders.

In this guide, I am going to help you understand and master how to effectively use relaxation techniques to your advantage. I will take you through the different proven and tested techniques to help in calming the mind. It's through these lessons that you will be able to find your Zen again. Ultimately, through the peace of mind that you will achieve, you will organize your life around it.

Over the years, I have had the privilege and honor to help people overcome stress and anxiety. I have helped and transformed the lives of hundreds of people through counseling and workshops. Indeed, this has been a humbling experience. One thing that I have learned through the years is that individuals don't know how to relax. Most people are simply aware of simple relaxing techniques that might not be as effective when faced with overwhelming levels of stress and anxiety.

While working with different clients, all with varying reasons for stress and anxiety, I have garnered sufficient knowledge to realize that some relaxation techniques are more effective than others. This manual will, therefore, provide you with insightful information concerning the relaxation techniques that will work best for you. Remember, this book doesn't just stop there, it will also help you put these techniques into practice. I use these techniques on myself and my family and I can assure that this guide will significantly improve your well-being and that of the people around you.

Once you've mastered how to use the relaxation techniques in this book, you will notice your life transform in ways you've never imagined before. You will regain your self-confidence and you will live a more relaxed life. Since you will effectively manage your daily stressors, there is a good chance that you will live a life full of abundance. We often stress because we approach life with a pessimistic attitude, thinking about what we lack or worrying that everything is crumbling down on us. A change of attitude will free you from this mindset. You'll stop feeling the annoying chest heaviness that often accompanies overthinking.

People's testimonies on how their lives have changed through my guided relaxation techniques have been the main motivation behind writing this book. In this guide, I will take you through different forms of relaxation techniques that have helped most of my clients. Plus, I will also explain to you how certain lifestyle choices can help you reduce stress. Most importantly, I will highlight proven ways of relaxing through physical meditation exercises and socializing.

Some of the relaxation techniques in this manual only require a few minutes of your time. Others might take up to 20-30 minutes, but they will help you fine-tune your entire life. You can make this guide your best friend to help you ease or lower your levels of anxiety and stress. I highly recommend that you go through all the relaxation techniques so that you find one that serves you best.

You must have heard that "old habits die hard?" Well... it's true, especially when it comes to your health and well-being. Human brains are like a sponge, and over time our brain will fill up with old and bad habits that are daunting to change and overcome. So, it's very important for you to teach yourself how to overcome the stress and anxiety that you suffer from, or you will miss out on the most valuable times of your life.

Living a happy life demands that you combine effective relaxation techniques alongside an optimistic attitude towards life. This wisdom is within you. Honing your ingrained life skills requires that you learn to trust your intuition. This will help you leverage on your power to transform your life. The time to change is NO W

Chapter 1: The Secrets Of Reacting To Stress And Anxiety

Stress and anxiety are difficult to avoid these days. There are numerous things that compete for your time and attention every day: it's hard to avoid stress even when you are having a good day. You might have had a positive attitude about how your day will turn out, but if traffic jams prevent you from arriving at work on time, this might cause you to be stressed. One phone call with bad news from a friend could also affect how you feel about the entire day. The point here is that stress is part of everyday life. The only thing you can do to ensure that stress doesn't affect your outlook towards life is to learn how to cope with it healthily.

Before you learn how to cope with stress, the first thing that you should strive to understand is the sources of your stress. It is by understanding your sources of stress and anxiety that you will be better placed to know how to react differently. There is a huge difference between how successful people react to stress and how others do. For instance, successful people understand that life has its ups and downs. When things are not going their way, they use this opportunity to learn from their bitter experiences. On the contrary, when things seem to work out, they use the opportunity to transform their lives for the better.

Evaluating How You React To Stress

Managing stress and anxiety is not easy. It's also not difficult. The only thing is that the effects of stress and anxiety might fail to portray themselves like other forms of diseases. This means that it might take you some time to accept that you're suffering from stress and anxiety-related disorders. Most people end up treating themselves for the wrong diseases while the root cause of their health issues is stress and anxiety. This is even true for weight-related issues: sometimes life can seem overwhelming and it can negatively affect your food choices. We all know how difficult it is to hit the gym when your mind is not at peace. Going for the morning jogs you were used to could suddenly seem impossible.

At the end of the day, stress and anxiety prevent you from taking action. They stop you from living the life that you've always wanted to live, robbing you of living a joyous life.

To overcome stress and anxiety, your first steps should be to identify your sources of stress. The reasons why you're stressed are different from why your friend feels like their lives are not turning out like they should, so it's very important that you never equate yourself to another individual. Plus, you never know if someone can manage their stressors better than you. As such, assuming that you're sailing on the same boat might give you the wrong impression about how you feel about yourself and the people around you.

Unfortunately, stress and anxiety management skills don't come out as you might have expected. If we all knew how to cope with stress and anxiety, there would be no need for you to read this guide. Stress management skills can be learned; you can also polish your existing skills to improve on how you manage stress.

To understand how you deal or react with stress, take a moment to evaluate yourself. People are different. Some folks turn a blind eye on the daily stress triggers that surround them. We often perceive these people as strong as it appears as though they never get stressed. In reality, everybody gets stressed. The only difference is that some of us have admirable stress management skills. So, the idea that there is a tight deadline coming up would not be a reason to be anxious or stressed for some of us.

Other people have poor stress management techniques.

For example, at the first glimpse of a stressful situation, your anxiety levels surge. You're running late for a meeting and you can't stop thinking about the previous warning your boss gave you. This leads to incessant negative thoughts. Will I get fired? Maybe this will affect my promotion! Why did I snooze my alarm? All these thoughts fill your mind and make you panic. These negative thoughts influence your decisions. Since you're thinking negatively, there is a good chance that you will make the wrong decisions. Ultimately, you may find yourself in a vicious cycle of negative thinking.

If you're not sure about how you react to stress, monitor yourself for a week. Note down the stress triggers that make you anxious. Take this opportunity to also note down how you respond.

What happens when you're dealing with pressure or a tight deadline at work? Does this aggravate you to the extent that you release your anger on your fellow workers, friends or loved ones? When having a bad day at work, one may want to carry their bad temper at home. If your partner provokes you when you're feeling as though you should be left alone, you may lash out with harsh words at them. Realize that it has little or nothing to do with the stress you're going through.

Stress can also make you overreact. Instead of understanding that your partner made a small mistake, you may want to make a mountain out of a molehill. This is something that many people in relationships struggle with. For instance, when going through a financial predicament, you could react if your partner spends money on something that you had not budgeted for. Sure, this is not the right thing to do. However, it's also not an excuse to pick a fight with your partner. There is a healthy way of responding to this to ensure that your relationship doesn't suffer under the strain.

Some people respond to stress by choosing to overeat. Research shows that stress can drive people to engage in "comfort eating." This is where people turn to foods that are high in sugar, calories, and fat (Jáuregui-Lobera & Montes-Martínez, 2020), leading to weight gain.

Chronic stress can also make you feel like there is too much to handle in your life. You may feel as though there is a lot of pressure from all corners. Your relationship is suffering, your career is on a downhill, and the people you call your friends might seem to care less. The truth is that your mind is suffering. Everything else around you is normal. If there is someone that needs to change, it's you.

Some people respond to stress by choosing to develop a negative mindset about everything. When you're stressed, this may have an impact on your perspective towards life and the people around you. For instance, instead of seeing good in things that happen around you, you may think differently. Even when good things are happening in your life, you may think that this will only last for a short time before something bad happens. Indeed, this is the worst way of responding to stress. As you might have guessed, it prevents you from seeing that life is full of abundance despite the challenges you're facing.

We also know of individuals who turn to drugs and alcohol when they are stressed. Studies reveal that there are millions of people who turn to alcohol and drugs when faced with stressful situations (Buddy T, 2016). Drinking might seem to provide you with some sense of relief. After a few glasses of whiskey, you may feel relaxed. However, it should be noted that this relief will only last for a short period. You won't have learned anything about managing your stressors or anxiety triggers. Worst, if your stress isn't taken care of, it could lead to overindulgence. This might lead to psychological and medical complications.

The way you react to stress has a huge impact on how you perceive your life and everything that is happening around you. But what causes you to be stressed or anxious in the first place? Let's look at some of the common stress and anxiety triggers.

The 4 Basic Sources of Stress and Anxiety

Studies reveal that there are approximately 33% of individuals who report feeling extremely stressed. The worst thing is that about 77% of people who feel stressed claim that it affects their physical health. 73% of individuals who suffer from stress claim that their mental health suffers a great deal (The Recovery Village, 2020).

In reality, there are many reasons why people suffer from stress. Depending on one's direction of thinking, anything can cause stress.

Take a moment to reflect on why you feel stressed today. Why are you in the position you are in today? What is it that you keep ruminating about? Maybe your financial situation is bothering you. It could be that your relationship is not turning out as expected or that you feel that you're not going anywhere with your partner. Your personal health issues might be the reason why you feel stressed. The family responsibilities on your shoulder could also make you feel stressed and overwhelmed. The point here is that there are numerous causes of stress. These causes can be categorized into 4 different sources.

Your Surrounding Environment

Stressors in your surroundings are termed as environmental stressors. These stressors can cause minor or major irritations in your everyday life. For instance, if you're working in a hot environment, the extreme temperatures can make you uncomfortable. The same case applies if you're working in a noisy environment. You may feel uncomfortable because your mind cannot think straight or you cannot hold a peaceful conversation with someone. Other environmental stressors include crowding, light, air quality, insects, war, tornadoes, and other natural disasters.

Your body reacts in a predictable manner when faced with a stressor. For instance, if you see a snake, your body will enter into the "fight-or-flight" response. The bodily response, in this case, is to "fight" the snake or "flight" - run away. This is what most people term as "adrenaline rush." Immediate threats like this example have less impact on your health as compared to long-term threats. If you keep experiencing a particular threat that makes you nervous from time to time, you may suffer the effects in the long run.

When your body enters the fight-or-flight response, it releases stress hormones such as norepinephrine and epinephrine. These chemicals are responsible for how your body responds when faced with a stressful situation. You may notice a sudden change in your heartbeat. Your palms could get sweaty and your hands could begin to shake. These physical changes are a result of the stress hormones that your body is releasing. It's important to understand that the frequent release of these hormones can affect your emotions. Your problem-solving ability will also be affected and you could even lose control of your bowels.

There are long term health effects that you could face if you constantly face environmental stressors that make your body enter into a fight or flight response. If you live in an environment prone to natural disasters, you're more likely to feel stressed or anxious. This happens because the stressors around you might be too much for the body's immune system to handle. Your blood sugar levels could spike up and you could face heart health issues. Frequent exposure to environmental stressors can contribute to mental health issues like anxiety, schizophrenia, and depression (Schimelpfening, 2015).

Social Stressors

The relationship with your social environment can also cause strain in your life. Social stress can include stress stemming from the struggles you go through at home, academic competition, friendship groups and so on. Even though social stress is not recognized as a major form of stress, it still ranks among the common forms of stress that people go through. One of the main causes of this type of stress is failure. Failure often leads to the loss of self-confidence and self-esteem. When one fails, they perceive themselves as though they have lost their social standing. Failure largely contributes to an increase in social stress because we live in a society where everybody yearns for approval. People usually characterize others based on how successful they are.

Another cause of social stress is the feeling of uncontrollability. Uncontrollability creates an environment where one feels like they have failed in life. It plants a seed of failure in the brain. When this happens, one feels paralyzed as they are unable to take desired actions in their lives that would lead to success. The effect of this is an increase in cortisol levels, a hormone responsible for helping you manage stress (Ana, 2018). In turn, the increase of cortisol levels in your body leads to decreased self-esteem.

If left untreated, the two causes of social stress will often lead to decreased self-esteem. This means that you will continue experiencing social stress and the effects are simply unbearable. When the brain is forced to frequently cope with social stressors, it releases several chemicals to help it cope with these stressful situations. Examples of these chemicals include dopamine, serotonin, and glutamate. When these chemicals are in present in the body in excessive amounts, it could lead to serious mental disorders (Ana, 2018). There are some physical illnesses which are caused by increased levels of social stress: certain cancers, ulcers, and cardiovascular disease.

So, how can you go about alleviating social stress? While there is no outright cure for it, there are a number of things that you can do to help yourself. An effective way of doing this starts with talking to the people that are close to you. If there are any broken relationships, fix them through regular communication. Indeed, we all know that there is power in sharing. A problem shared is a problem half solved. Talk to someone close to you about how you're feeling. This could help relieve some stress off your shoulders.

Another ideal way of dealing with social stress is by getting rid of toxic relationships. Toxic relationships are those relationships that negatively affect your mental and emotional state. Staying away from these relationships might help you improve your mental state.

While you can't "cure" social stress, the good news is that relief is attainable. The only thing you need to do is to open up and show that you're determined to relieve such stress in your life.

Physiological Stressors

Another source of stress that you may be experiencing is physiological. Just as the name suggests, this type of stressor relates to the physical aspects of your body. We cannot deny the fact that we are often stressed with our bodies. Many people will go to extremes to ensure that they lose weight or that their bodies look great. Statistics reveal that 62% of U.S. consumers who wish to eat a plant-based diet do to reduce weight. Only 17% of them do it to save money (Conway, 2018). Going by the numbers, this is a clear indication of what people are willing to do to ensure that they are physically fit.

As people grow older, they go through numerous physical changes. Sometimes these changes are difficult to cope with and thus, they could cause stress. For women, menopause brings a huge transition in their lives. Other triggers like lack of exercise, inadequate sleep, poor nutrition, aging, and injuries all tax the body. The manner in which you react to these changes can affect how you feel about yourself. If you think that you're gaining a lot of weight and there is little you're doing to remedy the situation, you may find yourself feeling stressed. If you continue going through the same feeling, it can take a huge toll in your life, leading to stressful symptoms like stomach upsets, muscle tension, anxiety, and headaches.

Your Thoughts

Have you ever stopped for a moment to consider the fact that everything you're thinking about is what you always attract into your life? In other words, you are the creator of your own little world. There are over 60, 000 thoughts that replay themselves in our minds daily. Experts believe that 90% of these thoughts are similar to what we were thinking about the previous day ("Destructive thinking: The hidden cause of stress," 2019). Interestingly, we can raise our awareness of these thoughts, but we often pay little attention to them.

The thoughts that replay themselves in our minds is what we call self-talk. When our minds replay these thoughts over and over, we begin to hold them to be true about ourselves. For instance, when your mind keeps telling you that you're wrong, chances are that you will always be skeptical about everything you do. How many times have you found yourself thinking, "Why do I keep making the same mistakes?" This is a mistaken belief that has replayed in your mind until you started believing it was true. Breaking away from this thought cycle is integral to your mental health. It's important that you realize that you're not your thoughts. These are just random thoughts in your mind and they hold nothing on you. Raising your awareness about your thoughts will help in mastering how to quieten your mind. More about this will be discussed in the following chapters.

How Stress Works

Your thoughts are a major source of stress. To clearly understand how stress works with regards to your thoughts, psychologist Albert Ellis used a model called the ABC stress model. This model argues that external events (A) are not the reason for your emotions (C), but your beliefs (B) are to be blamed (Selva, 2018).

Another way of looking into this is that our behaviors and emotions (C) are not directly influenced by our life events. Rather, they are influenced by the way we cognitively process and evaluate (B) these events.

This model goes further to point out that the way we respond to stress is not an unchangeable process. The manner in which events lead to beliefs that lead to certain consequences is not fixed. The issue here is that the type of *belief* that we choose to hold on to matters the most. As human beings, we have the power to change what we choose to believe. For that reason, we can manage stress by accepting the rational beliefs we have and disputing the irrational beliefs that mislead us.

To put it simply, changing your negative self-talk to a more optimistic self-talk can change your negative beliefs. Positive self-talk can help you cope with the challenges you face in life. Self-talk is the constant conversation that you have with your inner-self when no one is listening. Nobody can hear your self-talk apart from you. It's the voice of your thoughts speaking to you. There is power in these thoughts as they can make or break you. Positive self-talk will fill you with a positive mindset. It will fuel you to face life with courage. Negative self-talk, on the other hand, will aim to bring you down.

Once you become aware of your thoughts, you can learn to change your negative self-talk into positive. When faced with daily stressors, your mind can be filled with negative thoughts about the experiences you're going through. You might think that you're not perfect, that you have no control over your happiness, or that you cannot do it, or that asking for help is a sign of weakness, etc. Clearly, this is destructive thinking. You can change these thoughts by changing how you think. Ultimately, you will change how you respond to stress.

Behavioral Responses to Stress

Stress will affect your emotions. In turn, this means that your behavior will also change. Common behavioral symptoms that you will experience as a result of stress include changes in your appetite. Often, you will notice that you're either eating too much or too little. Avoiding responsibilities and procrastination is another common behavioral symptom of stress. Increased use of drugs and alcohol is also a behavioral change that will occur in most people. Nervous behaviors such as fidgeting, nail-biting and pacing can also be exhibited. When faced with stress, there are certain behavioral responses that would begin to take shape in your life.

Lack of Motivation

Stress should not be overlooked, especially with regards to unfulfilled goals and lack of motivation amongst people. Stress has shown to have a negative impact on motivation. In fact, scientists now believe that willpower is finite simply because its power can be affected by excessive levels of stress. It should be noted that sometimes the desire to succeed is closely tied to one's stress levels. Most people tend to think that motivation is a personality trait, and we tend to assume that people can't succeed because they lack motivation. In reality, motivation is more than just a personality trait. Despite the strong desire that one has to succeed, if they have a lot to deal with, their levels of motivation will be affected. When going through a lot of stress, motivation can simply fade away.

To clearly understand this, consider how a car operates. Assuming that a car uses willpower as fuel, every time the car meets a headwind, more fuel is required to propel it forward. The greater the resistance the car faces, the more willpower it uses. Now, if one is not satisfied with their work, for example due to the environment, the paycheck, or the daily tasks, all those factors all combine into a major source of discontentment, and an individual in such a situation will burn more willpower to cope.

When you keep using up your willpower every day, you will feel exhausted come nightfall. This leads to a situation where even small challenges will appear unbearable. It's imperative that you understand this clearly. Most people out there think that the people who cannot achieve their goals are lazy. You may have had the same thoughts about someone that has not accomplished their goals, or even about yourself. Yet, the reality is that stress may be responsible for sapping their motivation: stress is effectively standing between them and their vision or goals.

Change in Social Behaviors

Stress can also have a major impact on how you interact with the people around you. Normally, stress leads to social withdrawal. For instance, you might think that avoiding social gatherings is the best way of ensuring that people don't ask you questions about your career. Perhaps you feel that your career is not as good enough as compared to that of your friends. With this mentality, you could choose to disconnect.

Change in Sex Drive

Everyday stress can also have a major impact on your libido. Increased worry about deadlines at work, money, and other problems can lead to low libido. Unfortunately, this could be a major source of discontentment in your relationship. As discussed above, stress triggers the release of chemicals such as epinephrine and cortisol. These hormones should help your body deal with stress, but in excessive amounts, they will do more harm than good. Chances are that they will cause a reduction in your sex drive.

Stress and anxiety can affect your behavior, your thoughts, your feelings and your overall health. Being able to point out the common stress triggers that affect you helps to effectively manage your levels of stress and anxiety. From this chapter, you now realize that stress can cause a lot of harm in your life. You might blame the stars and luck because things are not working out for you. However, stress could be the main reason why you're suffering.

Chapter 2: General Tactics for Coping and Handling Stress

Before getting into the details about implementing effective relaxation techniques, it's important to tip you on the general tactics for coping with stress and anxiety. This chapter dives in to discuss the practical ways in which you can learn to cope with stress. Just to be clear, stress is nothing to joke with. There are millions of people out there who suffer in silence. Did you know that about 40 million adults in the United States suffer from stress and anxiety (Ducharme, 2018)? If you feel that life is weighing down on you because there's too much to handle, you're not alone. Follow the tips in this chapter to master how to deal with stress, especially in the fast-paced environment we live in today.

Practical Tips to Cope with Stress

Realize that You Cannot Control Everything

One way of coping with stress and anxiety is to admit that you have no control over everything. The only thing that you can do is change how you react towards situations that you encounter. Your relationship is not working out, maybe you're not the one to be blamed. Put your stress in perspective. Do you think it's as bad as you think? Maybe you're going through a financial quagmire because of the wrong decisions you made in the past. It has nothing to do with your personality. As such, you can choose to change how you react, for example, by choosing to accept responsibility for your mistakes and start making the right decisions from today.

Do Your Best

People often find themselves stressed because they have failed to accomplish their goals in life. When you feel that you've fallen short of your expectations, there is a likelihood that you will feel overwhelmed. Destructive thoughts will occupy your mind as you may think that you're not good enough. Cut yourself some slack! Who said that you should be perfect in everything that you do? Instead of aiming for perfection, strive for excellence. Be proud of your abilities and celebrate all the progress you make along the way. Remember, the point here is to build your confidence in positivity. Sure, things might not have turned out as you had planned, but you're proud of yourself because you did your best.

Maintain a Positive Attitude

An admirable aspect of successful people is that they understand how to leverage the power of positive thinking. These individuals stand out from the rest of us simply because they understand the power of their thoughts. The notion that you can change your world by changing your thoughts is just phenomenal. In fact, it seems too good to be true.

Maintaining a positive attitude is easy when everything is going your way. Your career is working out, your business is profitable, your relationships are fruitful, etc. All these good feelings can make you feel good about your life. On the contrary, when everything seems to be crumbling down on you, you may struggle to see anything positive about what is going on. Usually, it's at this point that your positive attitude is put to the test.

The notion of maintaining a positive attitude means that you should do your best to replace negative (destructive) thoughts with positive ones. With this positive mindset, you will always see the good in everything, whether good or bad. So, if your business is running on losses, you may consider this as an opportunity to learn something new about mitigating losses. If your marriage is on a rocky path, this could be an opportunity to renew your vows and remind each other how you feel. The idea here is that you should look for the good in everything that happens to you.

Identify Your Anxiety Triggers

It's not easy to solve a problem when you don't know the root cause of it. To effectively cope with stress, you should start by understanding your anxiety triggers. Is it your financial situation, your family, your work, or something else that is eating you up? Journaling how you feel every time you are stressed can help you identify potential anxiety triggers. This is because you will be better placed to point out existing patterns in how you react towards stress.

In the process of identifying the underlying causes of stress, try to categorize these reasons into three groups. First, classify the reasons you think you can find a solution. Secondly, group together the things that you think will get better with time. And third, put together the things you have no control over.

Once you're done with the above exercise, understand that you don't have to worry about the things in the second and third categories. For a start, some of these things will get better with time, so there is no reason for you to ruminate about them. On the other hand, some of the root causes of your stress are beyond your control. The best you can do to ensure that they don't affect you is by accepting things as they are and move on.

Limit Alcohol and Caffeine

Alcohol and caffeine are stimulants. This means that they can fuel your anxiety. High doses of caffeine and alcohol can increase your stress levels. If this continues, you may risk suffering from other mental health issues such as anxiety and depression. Drinking plenty of water can help in fighting the urge to consume coffee.

Eat Healthy

You are what you eat. Besides engaging in relaxation exercises, managing stress also requires you to eat healthy foods. Healthy foods provide the body with essential nutrients that would help in preventing negative effects of stress such as inflammation and oxidation. We also know that healthy foods contribute positively to maintaining a healthy weight.

The problem that most people face these days is that their tight schedules do not make it easy for them to prepare and eat healthy meals. It's easy for people to jump into fat-laden or sugar-rich foods as a way of treating themselves. As part of ensuring that you reduce or manage your stress levels, it is important that you develop a habit of eating healthy foods.

If you know that you might be tempted to turn to junk foods, embrace the idea of preparing your food at home. This reduces the likelihood of eating unhealthy meals. Of course, you will be more mindful of the meals you prepare. Hence, there is a good chance that you will eat healthy.

Exercise

Dieticians will often advise you that the best remedy to stress is exercising regularly. Putting physical stress on your body helps to alleviate mental stress and anxiety. There are several reasons behind this, including the fact that working out helps to lower the body's stress hormone like cortisol. Ultimately, you stand to benefit because the body will be releasing more of the feel-good chemicals (endorphins) that improve your mood. This is one of the main reasons why people feel good about themselves after exercising.

Another benefit of exercising is that it improves the quality of your sleep. After working hard at the gym or hitting the jogging trail, you will get better rest at night. Stress and anxiety can affect the quality of your sleep since your mind never stops thinking. One effective way of helping your mind to calm down is exercising. More about this will be detailed later in this guide.

Take Time Out

Sometimes the best way of coping with an overwhelming situation is to take some time out. You might push yourself to the limit hoping that things will work out fine, but in the end, you get the same results. All you need to do is to take a break. Stress can take a huge toll on you. In normal situations, people might see you as a loving and kind person. However, when you're stressed, all the positive traits that people see in you can fade away. Stress can, therefore, affect your relationships because it tends to mute your good personality traits.

It's crucial that you strike a balance between being responsible for other people and giving yourself some alone time. Realize that it's okay to take care of yourself from time to time. Self-care will go a long way in ensuring that you find yourself and cope with stress in a more reasonable manner. As such, consider taking some time to reflect and think about what you need and not what other people need from you. This is good for your mental and emotional health.

Practically, there are numerous ways of dealing with stress and anxiety. The most important thing to understand is that the way you react matters a great deal. There are situations where you might not have control over the problems you're experiencing. However, based on the ABC model you learned about in chapter 1, you have power over your thoughts. You can change what you choose to believe. Instead of believing that you cannot solve the problems at hand, realize that you have the power to reframe these problems. You can do this by viewing these problems from a positive perspective. Simply have a positive attitude towards the world around you and you will attract good things into your life.

Chapter 3: The Basics of Relaxation Techniques

You now understand the impact that stress and anxiety can have on your life. Chronic stress can put you at risk of suffering from health complications such as digestion issues, high blood pressure, anxiety, and depression, among others. Relaxation techniques are meant to help you enter into a calm state of mind. It's only when you're feeling calm that you are able to manage stress and reduce your anxiety levels. This chapter introduces you to the basic relaxation techniques that will be discussed in detail in this manual. In this section, you will understand what relaxation techniques are and the benefits that you should expect by practicing them regularly as advised.

What Are Relaxation Techniques?

Simply put, relaxation techniques refer to the strategies which are used to help in reducing levels of stress and anxiety (Star, 2012). It should be made clear that the relaxation techniques that will be discussed herein are not just meant to help you achieve a peaceful state of mind. These strategies are meant to guarantee that you manage stress and anxiety in a way that doesn't affect your health and wellbeing.

Perhaps you have been struggling with overwhelming levels of stress and anxiety and you might have been wondering whether there is a natural remedy to your condition. Relaxation techniques can help you free yourself from your mind. As previously discussed, one of the root causes of stress is your own thoughts. Accordingly, if you can master how you relax your mind, you can reduce stress and anxiety.

Your body will enter into a state of fight-or-flight when faced with stressful situations. In normal situations, this stress response is meant to help you deal with an environment where there is a potential threat. This means that some levels of stress and anxiety are good for the body. Chronic stress, on the other hand, is unhealthy. When dealing with this form of anxiety disorder, the stress response is activated frequently in the body. It causes unpleasant physical symptoms like increased heart rate, increased sweating, rapid breathing, and others.

Relaxation strategies have an opposite effect to that of the stress response. With the help of these techniques, your mind and body will be able to relax. Your heartbeat is lowered, bodily tensions reduced, and destructive thoughts decreased. Through the relaxation feeling that you will gain, you will garner an increased sense of self-worth and your problem-solving skills would be improved considerably.

Why Relaxation is So Important

Perhaps you are wondering: why is relaxation so important? Where do I get the time to relax? If someone told you that you need to relax, the first question that you would want to ask them is where do you get the time to relax? Maybe you're always on the go, doing what you can to ensure that your kids have a bright future. Indeed, the hustle and bustle of life have put us in a situation where we think that being busy is the only way to succeed. The fast-paced environment that we live in has blinded us from realizing the importance of taking some time to relax.

We often forget the importance of stepping away from the things that contribute to our stress and anxiety levels. What we fail to realize is that such relaxation bestows us with the energy we need to handle our daily stressors. It's important to reiterate the fact that not all stress is bad. Mild stress can push us into doing something that is beneficial for ourselves. However, going through high levels of stress frequently can pose detrimental effects to our mental, physical, and emotional health.

Stress overload can result in physical symptoms such as tension in the shoulders and neck, headaches, fatigue, dizziness, poor sleep patterns, etc. Since the brain will be releasing cortisol hormone more often, your mental state also stands to be affected. You will often find yourself worrying too much, overthinking things beyond proportion, having trouble making decisions and being afflicted with poor concentration. You likely feel like you've lost control of your thoughts and that your mind is controlling you. Emotionally, you will feel burdened with lots of anxiety and diminished self-esteem. This could lead to depression. Your behavior will also change since you lack control of your thoughts and emotions. People may find you aggressive or, anti-social, or you may indulge in self-destructive behavior like abusing drugs and alcohol.

Every time you put your body and mind in a state of relaxation, you increase the flow of blood around your body. This means that energy is spread through all corners of your system. The benefit gained here is that you will have a more calm and clearer mind that is able to make the right decisions at the right time. The more you make the right decisions, the more you build your life on positivity. Relaxation reduces your blood pressure by lowering your heart rate. In turn, this relieves tension in your body. With the increased blood flow throughout your system, digestion will also improve.

Normally, when your body and mind are stressed, this results in abnormal behavioral and emotional responses. You could be angered by a petty issue just because you're stressed. It's also easy to get frustrated when things don't turn out as you had expected. Relaxation reduces the likelihood of these experiences happening. With the clear state of mind that you will attain, you will be better placed to react well to stress and anxiety. You will be more aware of your thoughts. This results in a mindful way of approaching the daily challenges that seem to weigh you down.

There is a big difference between relaxing at the end of the day while staring at the TV or browsing through your social media pages and practicing relaxation strategies that will be discussed in this guide. Relaxation demands that you should change your pace of life. Activities that will help you relax include using relaxation techniques such as deep breathing, visualization, progressive muscle relaxation, physical meditation, and body scan. These relaxation strategies are helpful since they bring your mind and body in a state of true inner peace.

Prepare Your Mindset

The concept of relaxation might sound easy, but most people will still struggle when told to relax their bodies and minds. The tricky aspect of relaxation is that it requires you to refocus your mind. Of course, there are certain things that you may be worried about on a regular basis. Maybe you're stressing over work or family problems. Financial challenges that you may be experiencing could fill your mind with destructive thoughts about your future. For you to reap the health benefits of relaxation, it's crucial that you refocus your mind off these issues. You should picture yourself feeling happy and grateful for the good things that you have or you anticipate having.

You may have the impression that refocusing your mind is challenging because there is a lot going on in your life. Well, this is where our guided meditation will help you. Breathing and physical meditation techniques will help you listen to your thoughts and refocus them.

The relaxation techniques discussed in this guide are meant to help you transform your life in general. But before this happens, you have to develop a positive mindset towards what you will be doing. Think about the pain that you have been through all these years or the past few months/weeks. Maybe life has pushed you to the point where you feel like giving up. You might have been feeling like everything is a struggle. You've always been working hard and nothing seems to work out. It could also be that your personal issues have been weighing you down and this has affected all facets of your life..

As previously noted in chapter 1, stress can quickly extinguish your motivation. The mere fact that you haven't achieved your goals doesn't mean that you're lazy or unlucky. Stress and anxiety could be the root cause of all the problems that you're going through. It is for this very reason that before you start practicing the relaxation techniques in this guide you need to ensure that you know your goal.

Develop a positive mindset towards everything that you would be doing to ensure that you manage your stress and lower your anxiety levels. You should realize that the journey towards achieving a peaceful state of mind might not be easy from the get-go. Nevertheless, it is through your continued practice of these relaxation techniques that you will master how to put your body and mind in a state of tranquility.

So, expect your mind to wander from time to time. You've never done this before. As such, it's normal for your mind to think about negative things when you're trying to focus on the positive. When this happens, you should increase your awareness of your thoughts and recognize that your mind is roaming. This is what breathing and body scan techniques will teach you. It's okay to make mistakes while practicing the relaxation techniques for the first few times. Sure, you might not do it right as recommended in the manual, so aim to improve but don't beat yourself up about it. Strive to achieve a calmer state of mind each time you practice the relaxation techniques in this book. If you focus on daily improvement, rest assured that you will master how to relax your body and mind and benefit from it.

Finding Time to Relax

In line with the idea of relaxation, we cannot overlook the concept of time. Most people will jump into the idea of relaxation with the hope that they will find it easy to remember to practice relaxation techniques every day. The joy of trying out a new challenge might inspire you to start on a high note. Then life happens, and you suddenly realize that you don't have time to engage in these relaxation techniques daily as you might have wanted.

This is the same thing that happens to people when they start exercising. At the beginning, things appear interesting simply because you're doing something new. With time, the exhilaration fades away. Before you know it, you're prioritizing other mundane things over exercising. It's not until later that you again realize that exercising is important for your mind and body.

In reality, life can get busy. Usually, the demands of life can blind us from realizing that it's important to take some time off to unwind and relax. This makes it very important to find ways of fitting relaxation strategies into your tight schedule. Don't just assume that you will practice relaxation techniques in the morning and in the evening. It's vital that you reorganize your life to guarantee that you have time to practice the relaxation techniques that will be discussed in this guide. If you want to reap the benefits of these techniques in just 7 days, consistency is key.

So, how do you find time to relax?

Record How You Spend Time

The secret to finding time for your relaxation practice is to record how you use time. Start by evaluating your schedule to determine whether there are certain activities that rob you of your precious time. With the digitized environment that we live in, there are plenty of "time thieves" that you can point to. Some of these thieves include the television, the internet, and even toxic people. For instance, you may not realize that you spend more than 40 minutes every day browsing through your social media pages. Why don't you consider allocating this time to relax? After all, some of the relaxation techniques in this guide take less than 30 minutes.

Outsource Activities

Another effective way of finding some relaxation time is by outsourcing some activities. There are times where we are too busy to realize that we cannot do everything ourselves. Delegating tasks can help you gift yourself some free time to practice self-care through relaxation strategies.

Learn to Say No

It's also important to learn to say no to some of the tasks that are assigned to you. Don't take on tasks that you cannot handle. You may think that saying no is offensive, but from a positive perspective, saying no also means giving yourself some free time. You can use this time to relax your body and mind as a way of coping with stress and anxiety.

Focus on Your Breath

Despite all your efforts to find the time, you might realize that you actually don't have time at all. Well, guess what? You can practice breathing relaxation techniques in just a few minutes. You can take a few minutes in a quiet place and focus on your breath for less than 5 minutes. The good thing is that you can also do this even while in a tense environment. More about this will be discussed in detail later in this guide.

Unplug

Most individuals who are used to browsing through the internet think that this is the best way to kill time and relax. Unfortunately, the information that you feed your mind through these pages does more harm than good. Instead of picking your smartphone to browse, why don't you use this time to practice the breathing exercise that serves you best? At the end of the day, you would have lowered your stress levels and you will feel more energized and ready to tackle any challenges that pop up.

Win Your Day in the Morning

Start your day on a positive note by waking up early. The advantage of waking up early is that you get some extra hours to engage in activities that you wouldn't have found time to do later in the day. In this case, you should make a habit of meditating in the morning. This allows you to win your day in the morning. Starting your day on a good note with positive affirmations can help you achieve more in life. With this mindset, you can effectively manage stress better.

Make an Appointment - With Yourself

It's also imperative that you schedule in your "me-time." Consider your relaxation time as any other important appointment that you need to attend to. Noting down that you have an appointment with yourself will increase the likelihood of engaging in the activity. Remember, you're the one to benefit from the relaxation strategies that will be looked at. You've been suffering for too long in silence and it's time to overcome your anxiety and stress. Commit yourself to the process and you will reap the benefits in just a few days.

Now that you understand what relaxation techniques are and their relevance, let's move on to the next chapter where you start preparing yourself for the first relaxation strategy. It's important that you read chapter 3 before moving to chapter 4. You have to develop the right mindset to allow the relaxation techniques to help you. Without this, it would be difficult for you to notice any change in terms of relaxing your mind and body. When this happens you might be discouraged since the techniques discussed might not work. For that reason, mental preparation is key to ensuring that you reap the benefits of taking time to relax.

Chapter 4: The Examination Phase; Be Your Own Doctor

Usually, before a doctor can determine what you're suffering from, they will consider the symptoms that you're experiencing. Your symptoms will help them ensure that you're provided with the right medication. In the same way, managing stress and anxiety requires that you understand the symptoms that you're displaying. Symptoms of stress will vary from one person to the other. This is because people cope with stress differently. Some people might consider certain symptoms as mild. Others might find similar symptoms as overwhelming. Accordingly, it's important to understand how stress affects you from a personal perspective.

This chapter requires you to examine yourself as you strive to understand how stress affects your body and your overall well-being. This personal assessment is meant to help you become aware of your thoughts, emotions, behavior, and reactions to your immediate environment. To help you perform this self-assessment, we will define some of the signs and symptoms of stress overload.

Signs and Symptoms of Stress Overload

Cognitive Symptoms

Stress can be something that occurs to you more frequently than not. Chances are that you find yourself constantly worrying about your future or the mistakes you've made in the past. It could also be that you're not certain about what's going on in your life. Your friends and family might have pointed out to you that you always seem stressed. In reality, stress can cause numerous problems in your life, especially with regard to your cognitive abilities. The following are cognitive symptoms that will indicate that you need to manage stress before it causes more harm to your life.

Constant Worry

Do you often find yourself worrying about things that haven't happened yet? Maybe you keep thinking about "What if?" What if things go wrong in the near future? If you find yourself asking these questions, then you're stressed. Individuals who constantly worry increase their anxiety levels. In turn, this contributes to increased levels of stress. While it's okay to worry about something, excessive worry can affect your mental health. People who constantly worry will even worry when things are running smoothly.

Forgetfulness

You may also find yourself forgetting about important things in your daily routine. If this is the case, it could be an indication that you're dealing with stress overload. At work, you could find yourself forgetting about important projects that ought to have been completed. The same thing will affect your personal life as you might forget crucial family events. Forgetting things is normal. Nevertheless, in extreme cases, it can cost you your job or your relationships.

Disorganization

If you notice that people around you are complaining about your disorganized way of life, they could be pointing you to a red flag that you're stressed. When you're disorganized, you could find yourself misplacing things that are important to you. In fact, you may also mistakenly get rid of items that are essential. Your disorganized nature could also influence how you prioritize tasks. Ultimately, this will affect your productivity.

Trouble Focusing

Do you struggle to focus on a single task or activity? When you're stressed, there is a lot going on in your mind. As such, mental clutter will prevent you from concentrating. If you cannot focus on one task at a time, you will definitely struggle to finish tasks on time. Your productivity will be affected and this will lead to more stress.

Racing Thoughts

If you notice that your mind can't seem to calm down, then this is another sign of stress. Racing thoughts can affect your decision-making abilities. One minute you're thinking about doing something and the next minute your mind is thinking about a different thing. This can prevent you from taking any action because you're not sure of the right thing to do. Often, such indecisiveness leads to stress and anxiety. At the end of the day, you may choose to do nothing because you're too afraid of making mistakes. The problem is that failing to take action only contributes to more and more stress piling up. Accordingly, if you feel that your mind is constantly racing with all kinds of thoughts, this could be a sign of distress.

Poor Judgement

People who are stressed are more likely to make the wrong decisions simply because they feel overwhelmed. When there is a lot going in your life, you may want to say yes to everything just to get people out of your way. Since you will be making hasty decisions, chances are that you will make the wrong judgment calls that would affect your personal and professional life. In most cases, you will find that you keep regretting making certain decisions. This happens because you never gave things a second thought to determine whether you were making the right decision or not.

Pessimistic Outlook

Individuals who suffer from chronic stress tend to focus only on the negative. Stress can make your life miserable. Since your mind is filled with destructive thoughts, it's difficult to notice anything good in whatever happens to your life, and you will always expect the worst to happen. Your motivation will fade away since you have a pessimistic outlook towards things. Therefore, you will expect to fail in everything that you do. Of course, you cannot succeed if you keep focusing on negativity.

Psychological and Emotional Symptoms

Stress can also affect your psychological and emotional wellbeing. Some of the signs to look out for are succinctly discussed in the following lines.

Depression

Stress can also manifest to you in the form of a persistent or severe low mood. This is what the Anxiety and Depression Association of America (ADAA) defines as depression. There is a strong correlation between high levels of stress and the early stages of depression. If you feel that you're always feeling low, it is a clear sign that you're stressed.

Anxiety

Anxiety is where you are faced with overwhelming dread. You might not be sad, but you are feeling overwhelming fear about what might happen. This is where you fill your mind with "what ifs" questions. The issue here is that you dread things that you create in your mind. You might be worried thinking that you will get fired or that your spouse will leave you. These are just destructive thoughts occupying a lot of space in your mind. Constant worry can ultimately lead to stress.

Tension

Tension is also another common symptom of stress. While some tension is considered helpful, constant tension can ultimately contribute to increased levels of stress. Usually, tension can arise if you're dealing with a difficult relationship. Maybe you're always clashing with your partner. Too much competition around you can also make you tense more often. In this regard, instead of doing things normally, tension can make you feel as though there is a lot of pressure to deal with. At the end of the day, this will affect your performance.

Some reasonable level of tension is helpful. It's there to encourage you to take the necessary steps in saving a situation. If there is a strain in your relationship, tension should motivate you to take corrective measures to resolve the issue. Tension should be a short-term feeling that disappears after some time. If you find yourself feeling constantly tensed, then it shows that you need to make major changes in your life.

Insecurity

You might also feel insecure because of the varying psychological signs of stress. When you feel insecure, it may affect how you think about yourself. For instance, you might end up thinking that you add no value to the world around you. At work, you could think that you're underperforming.

Harsh self-judgment and unhelpful comparisons could make you feel inferior to the people around you. Individuals who suffer from stress will struggle appreciating what they have or what they are capable of achieving. Usually, this is what contributes to insecurity.

At times when things appear to be getting out of control, it's easy for one to believe that they are responsible. This can undermine your self-worth. It should be noted that self-worth is not necessarily defined by what you achieve. Rather, it's defined by who you are. Raising your self-esteem helps ensure that you build courage towards such psychological symptoms of stress.

Disengagement

To be honest, there are times when we all feel like we are not motivated to work. It's a normal experience to go through. After all, you cannot be motivated 24/7. However, in other cases, such a lack of motivation may spin out of control. You may constantly feel like the job you are doing is just there to help you earn something at the end of the day. This negative feeling could lead to disengagement.

There are also situations where you find yourself falling behind in the expectations that you had set for yourself. Maybe you had planned to achieve something in two or three months, but you fell short. So, you strive to do more with the hopes of catching up. Gradually, this leads to disengagement from life. You begin focusing too much on work as you spare little time to make real connections, finding less time to engage in activities that you love.

In terms of work, it gets to a point where you lose focus on what's important. You become obsessed with revenue, income, or the quantity of work you deliver. Indeed, this is what is termed as disengaging. One of the most important things that you can lose in life is purpose. You lose purpose in what you do. As you lose touch with people who would have made life meaningful to you, you find no joy in doing what you do. You end up feeling like your life is a constant vicious cycle where you're not achieving anything.

In extreme cases, you may ask yourself, "What's the point of doing all this if I am not going to be happier?" The truth is that you need to re-engage with life. This means making meaningful connections with the people around you. In a way, this will help you create your own happiness.

Isolation

Your job or other life situations may also leave you feeling isolated from time to time. This might make you feel left out. If there are problems that you may be going through, you could feel like there is no one to talk to or that no one can help you. The problem with repeated isolation is that it could make you drift away from people. Bit by bit you lose connections with important people in your life. This might go on until it gets to a point where you feel like you need to open up to someone and you have no one to turn to.

Unfortunately, the people around you might not notice that you're absent. This is because people are too busy dealing with their own problems.: they might mean no harm but you may be suffering in silence.

Psychological symptoms can affect your life in many ways. The problem with these symptoms is that they are difficult to notice. People around you might not realize that you're suffering simply because they cannot see or understand the inner workings of your mind. It's only when you open up to others that they will be able to help you.

Behavioral Symptoms

Problems are easily solved if you can identify their root cause. The same principle applies when you're dealing with stress. Your behaviors can also help you identify if you are suffering from stress. Compared to psychological and cognitive symptoms of stress, behavioral symptoms can easily be identified. The people around you might also notice your change of behavior due to stress. This doesn't mean that you should wait for people to tell you that your behavior has changed. As part of ensuring that you enjoy life, it's crucial that you heighten your awareness of likely behavioral symptoms. Some of these symptoms are described as follows.

Sleeping Difficulties

Getting a good night's sleep often requires one to relax. If you keep ruminating about the past and the future, this can leave you feeling worried and anxious. It may be challenging to shut down your brain and go to sleep. It's for this reason that people who are stressed will often toss and turn all night.

Life as we know it is quite challenging. People have a lot of pressure to deal with every day. Normally, people go the extra mile of sacrificing their sleep to ensure that they meet their goals and aspirations. Getting fewer hours of sleep might appear as the best way of keeping pace with your daily activities. Nevertheless, the importance of sleep to your optimal health should not be ignored.

Failure to get the right amount of sleep can affect your productivity the following day. You will feel tired and chances are that you might want to skip some important activities just because you need to rest. If you continue suppressing your sleep, there is no denying the fact that you will lag behind in your performance. This will contribute to increased levels of stress. You can't seem to get things done on time. Negative emotions will take a huge toll on you and stress will keep mounting.

Lack of Productivity

Timekeeping becomes a huge problem when an individual is stressed. The issue here is that you might overwhelm yourself by taking on too many tasks that you cannot handle. You could also avoid tasks since you are trying to avoid responsibility. Procrastination could also be the reason why you keep pushing tasks until the last minute. This is a common trait of people who are stressed.

It should be made clear that your poor time management skills might not explicitly imply that you're stressed. If you've been managing time well and all of a sudden you notice that you waste a lot of time, this could be an indication that something is not right. Maybe you're finding it a challenge to keep up with some tasks that you used to find easy to handle. Sometimes you may even feel like you're overloading yourself with things you cannot handle. Your lack of productivity should be well checked as it could indicate that you're dealing with stress.

Withdrawal

Stress will have a significant impact on your self-confidence and self-esteem. When you're stressed, coping with social situations becomes a major issue. Avoidance behavior will slowly creep in and you will do your best to avoid social situations to protect your fragile self-esteem.

Sometimes you may not even notice that you're withdrawing because you tend to assume that it's a common thing to do. For instance, your friends might invite you for lunch but you may choose to avoid going because you think that you cannot cope with a large group of people. You may also avoid work because you don't trust yourself to handle a particular task. Such signs of withdrawal should not be taken lightly. They are an indication that you're likely dealing with stress and anxiety.

Exhaustion

A person who is stressed will often feel like they are running from one emergency situation to another. This means that they may not find enough time to rest. If you constantly feel fatigued, it could be an indication that you're feeling overwhelmed and that you're stressed.

Addictive Behavior

Individuals who are stressed might live in denial for too long. They might not realize that they are stressed until it's too late to turn back. In situations where individuals are unaware that they are stressed, they could resort to short-term solutions to help them feel good. They may turn to drugs and alcohol looking for relief. What people may fail to realize is that such short term solutions have harmful long term consequences.

The idea of turning to drugs and alcohol as a way of dealing with stress should be the last thing on your mind.

If you drink or use drugs to escape from a situation that you don't want to handle, then you have a dependency issue. You should realize that it's better to face your problems than drowning them in alcohol or any other drugs. Your problems will not go away just because you chose to ignore them. In fact, the more you keep ignoring them, the bigger the problems get. Ultimately, you will want to drink more to free your mind from having to think about the problem. This is where you become addicted.

Unhealthy Eating Habits.

Stress also drives people to seek comfort in what they eat. Most people will want to snack on unhealthy foods since they provide temporary relief to a bad feeling that one might have been going through. It's that good feeling that you get when you eat French fries that makes you want to eat more of them when you're feeling down. These foods are not nutritious, and such overindulgence can lead to health-related diseases such as high blood pressure, obesity, and heart disease among others.

People respond differently to stress. While some might overeat, others will avoid eating. Usually, this happens when individuals have negative perceptions of their self-image. It can also occur when they have negative attitudes towards food. Whatever the reasons that you might have to avoid food, devastating effects can be felt if this is left unchanged.

There is a good reason why you're always advised to eat right. Eating healthy foods provides your body with important nutrients for optimal functioning, while unhealthy foods stop you from performing at your best. Think about it this way, when you eat healthy foods, you feel good about yourself. You know that you have made the right decision and this evokes some good feelings. Eating unhealthy foods, on the other hand, makes you worry. You may be worried that you will slowly gain weight or suffer any negative effects of your bad eating habits.

This chapter has opened your eyes to the realization that you can be your own doctor. This means that you can perform a self-evaluation test before turning to the relaxation techniques that will be described in this guide. It is very important that you understand the significance of knowing the stress symptoms that you display. Arguably, by raising your awareness of these symptoms, you will be better placed to effectively manage your stress. This is something that you can do every time you notice that you're showing some of the signs that have been discussed herein.

Don't allow stress and anxiety to weigh you down while you can utilize the relaxation techniques outlined in this guide to manage your situation. You deserve to be happy and you owe it to yourself to use relaxation techniques to calm your mind and find inner peace.

Chapter 5: Breathing Techniques Guide

Take a deep breath in. Pause for a second and let it out. How do you feel after that? You may notice that there is a sudden relief that your body goes through with such deep breathing. Breathing exercises are a powerful tool to help you ease your stress and anxiety. Making these exercises part of your daily routine can make a huge difference in your ability to manage stress and lower your levels of anxiety.

In this chapter, you will garner insights on how to use breathing to increase your awareness of your inner self. You will also learn how to use these breathing exercises to release tension in your body and relax. More importantly, you will know how to reduce or relieve symptoms of stress.

Introduction to Breathing

Every day there are certain activities on our to-do list that we consider normal. We tend to think about some of these activities frequently, for example, eating and drinking. In fact, if you're thirsty, you might be thinking about finding a glass of water. The same case applies if you're hungry. You may be thinking about your next meal.

Remarkably, there are certain things that we do every single day, yet we don't think about them at all. When was the last time you thought about how you're breathing? Maybe this is something that you never think about unless you have a bad cold or you engage in long-distance running. Often, people take breathing for granted. The interesting thing about life is that it goes on even when you're not conscious about it.

Breathing is integral for your survival. Your life depends on it. With each breath you take, you breathe in life: you take oxygen into the body and release carbon dioxide as the waste product.

Your lungs are the organs responsible for your breathing. The lungs are part of the respiratory system. You may not see your lungs, but you can easily feel them at work each time you breathe in and out.

Place your hands on your chest. Take a deep breath in and out. As you breathe in, your chest expands. As you breathe out, your chest returns to its usual size. The expanding and contracting of your chest is because of your lungs in action.

You know how to breathe, but chances are that you might not be making maximum use of your lungs. Unfortunately, this leaves you wasting away every breath of extra energy that you would have taken advantage of. You're not alone. Most people are never conscious of their breathing. In the modern day, poor breathing habits are quite common. As previously noted, it is very likely that you've never thought about the intimate relationship that exists between your breathing, your mind, and your body.

It is worth pointing out that by being conscious of your breathing, you have the power to transform and strengthen both your mind and your body. Human beings are capable of transforming themselves to a degree that beats scientific understanding. Unfortunately, modern life has pushed people to extremes and they take their breathing for granted. People are rushing day and night to earn a living and this has disconnected us from our bodies. The negative effect experienced here is that we obliviate the peaceful and deep breathing gift we were bestowed with at birth.

Fortunately, it's never too late to start listening to your body. The breathing exercises discussed herein should help you reconnect with your body and mind, and reap the benefits of the calmness you gain.

Effectiveness of Breathing in Relieving Symptoms of Stress and Anxiety

Breathing exercises are a great tool to get more in touch with your body, mind and spirit. Conscious breathing can help in bringing your mind to the present moment. Equally, such breathing can help bring your attention to the energy of your emotions. When negative emotions seem to weigh you down, conscious breathing can increase your awareness of these emotions and how they are affecting you.

Every time you are stressed, the negative energy from your emotions can take a huge toll on you. It affects how you feel, react, and how you make decisions. With the help of deep conscious breathing, you can shift your attention from the negative energy in your body. This helps in releasing the weight of these emotions which can be quite debilitating. There are other benefits to conscious breathing, including the fact that it helps increase oxygen flow and alertness. Your body can also detoxify more readily when you practice breathing repeatedly during the day. Although breathing is considered as the most natural thing to do, it's also a skill that you improve with constant practice.

Mastering the Art of Breathing

There is nothing new about breathing exercises. The only thing that you will be doing here is breathing consciously while listening to your body and mind. The benefits of breathing can be experienced immediately, or it might also take some time for you to notice a change in how you feel or how you think. With constant practice, you start reaping the benefits of conscious breathing. The goal of this guide is to ensure that you reap the benefits of breathing in 7 days or less: it's very important that you develop a daily breathing program that serves you best.

Instructions

This section is divided into three categories to ensure that you find it easy to master the art of breathing. The first thing that we will discuss is the preparation. How do you prepare yourself to breathe? What steps should you take to ensure that you realize the benefits of such breathing? Most importantly, how do you prepare yourself mentally for the process?

Next, we will look into the breathing basics. Here we will take a look at the two types of breath; chest breathing and diaphragmatic breathing. The last section will focus on breathing exercises to increase your awareness and release tension from your body.

Preparation Phase

Conscious breathing demands that you choose an appropriate time and place where you will not be disturbed. Since you're in the learning stages, it is crucial that you practice breathing in a quiet place. You should also perform these breathing exercises at the same time daily. This will make it easier for you to develop a habit that you can stick to. After mastering the art, you can breathe anywhere, especially if you find yourself in a tense situation.

As you prepare to practice breathing every day, it's important to use your nose and not your mouth. Therefore, if your nasal passages are blocked, you should find a way of clearing them. In instances where you cannot clear them, use your mouth.

Choose a relaxed position that is best for you. Depending on your purpose for breathing, you can settle in different positions. For instance, if your aim is general relaxation, breathe while seated. If you intend to soothe yourself to sleep, the best position would be lying down.

Good posture is key to ensuring that you relax your body and mind. Don't just assume any seated position. Strive for a comfortable position where your spine is well supported and your arms and legs are stretched out.

As a beginner, consider practicing breathing while lying down. This is because it's easier for you to relax your body and mind while in this position. Gradually, you can try breathing while seated. But give yourself enough time for you to master how to calm your body and mind while in this position.

There are two positions that you can assume while lying down. You can either lie down with your knees bent or with your legs stretched out and slightly apart. Nevertheless, the best position is with your knees slightly bent, because it offers you a relaxed body posture, making it easy to calm your mind while you focus on breathing.

It's important that you choose a relaxed position that suits you. Before beginning the exercise, take a few moments to scan through your body to determine whether you've assumed the right posture. While doing this, relieve tension from your body as you shift for the best position. The point is to make yourself as comfortable as possible.

Breathing Basics

How Do You Breathe?

1. First, it's important to evaluate how you currently breathe. To do this, start by closing your eyes, then put your left arm

on your abdomen near the waistline. Put your right arm on your chest, at the center.

2. Pay attention to how you breathe without changing anything. The point here is to notice how air is moving in and out of your body through your nose (or through your mouth.)

3. Raise your awareness of how air is filling your lungs when you breathe in. Again, observe how air is moving out of your lungs as you breathe out.

4. As you breathe in and out, notice the movement of your hands. Which hand moves up and which one moves down?

If the hand placed on your abdomen (left arm) rises the most compared to the one on the right, then you're breathing diaphragmatically. Conversely, if the hand on your chest moves more, then you're chest breathing.

Diaphragmatic Breathing

The diaphragm refers to a large, dome-shaped muscle that is situated at the base of the lungs. Using the diaphragm correctly to breathe helps you benefit from the breathing exercises (Diaphragmatic breathing exercises & techniques, n.d.). With diaphragmatic breathing, the abdominal muscles are used to provide more power to the diaphragm muscle so that it can efficiently empty your lungs.

So, what is diaphragmatic breathing? Basically, this refers to a type of breathing intended to ensure that you use the diaphragm correctly while breathing. This results in benefits such as:

- Strengthening of the diaphragm
- Decreased oxygen demand
- Less effort and energy required to breathe
- Slowing your breathing rate

Mastering The Technique

1. Assume a lying position either in your bed or on a flat surface.

2. Use a pillow to support your head and your knees so that you take on a lying position with your knees bent.

3. Place your left hand on your chest and the right hand just below the rib cage. This position will allow you to notice how the diaphragm moves while you breathe in and out.

4. Now, take a deep breath in slowly through your nose. As you breathe in, notice how the hand on your abdomen rises. Ensure that you don't move the hand on your chest.

5. Exhale through your nose. You can also breathe out through your pursed lips. This allows you to slow down the rate of your breathing.

6. Once you know how to use this technique, you can slow down the rate of your breathing. This can be done through your conscious effort in knowing that you're paying attention to your breath. You don't have to frown while performing this

breathing exercise. Relax. Smile. Notice the body movements as you breathe in and out. Listen to your body. As you breathe out through your pursed lips, pay attention to the sound and feel of warm air as it leaves through your lips.

7. Feelings, sensations, and all kinds of thoughts might flow into your mind and this could distract you. Don't resist. Notice the presence of these thoughts and emotions and gently bring back your focus on your breathing.

8. Breathe diaphragmatically for about 5-10 minutes.

9. At the end of this exercise, pause for a moment to reflect on how you feel.

It's highly recommended that you scan through your body at the start and at the end of the exercise. This gives you the opportunity to compare how you felt before and how you feel after the exercise.

As a novice breather, it's recommended that you perform the diaphragmatic breathing while lying down. Once you've practiced enough, you can practice breathing while sitting on a chair.

Diaphragmatic Breathing on a Chair

1. Find a comfortable chair to sit on. Your knees should be bent with your back, shoulders, and neck relaxed.

2. Place your hands on your chest and on your rib cage just as you did in the above exercises.

3. Take a deep breath in slowly through your nose. While doing this, notice how your hands are moving.

4. Exhale through your nose or through your pursed lips.

5. Remember to focus on your breathing as you strive to notice your thoughts, emotions and sensations that come to you. The goal is to bring your mind to focus on your breathing regardless of what you may be feeling or thinking.

Note: At first, diaphragmatic breathing might not be easy for you. In fact, you may get tired during your first few attempts. However, it's very important that you continue practicing as it gets better with time.

So, how often should you practice this type of breathing? Start by practicing this breathing exercise for about 5-10 minutes. This can be done 3-4 times daily. With time, increase the amount of time to about 20 minutes. Once you're good at it, you can place a book on your abdomen while your hands lie stretched on either side.

Breathing for Increased Awareness and Tension Release

Mindful Breathing for Increased Awareness

Mindfulness breathing is another breathing exercise that you can utilize to increase your awareness and bring your mind to the present moment. Basically, mindfulness breathing is about focusing on your breathing. This exercise can be done standing or lying down. The point is to find a comfortable position where you will easily concentrate without getting distracted. Your eyes can be open or closed when performing this exercise. However, to ensure that you don't struggle to focus, closing your eyes is highly recommended.

With regards to time, it helps a lot to schedule your mindful breathing exercise. When you set some time aside to practice this exercise, it means that you will be doing it consciously, but this should not stop you from practicing it when you're feeling anxious or stressed during the day.

When faced with a stressful situation, make a deliberate effort to take an exaggerated breath. Inhale through your nose and pause for about 2 seconds. Exhale through your mouth while allowing all the air that you had inhaled to leave via your pursed lips. While you're inhaling and exhaling, notice any body changes without trying to change anything. For instance, pay attention to the rising and falling of your chest or the feeling of your nostrils as air moves in and out. Your mind might wander while you're doing this. It's okay. Don't resist it. Rather, notice this happening and gently shift your focus back to your breath.

To help you find it easy to practice mindfulness breathing, below are steps that you should follow.

1. Find a quiet place where you can practice mindfulness breathing without interruptions. Make yourself comfortable by either sitting on the floor or on a chair. If you choose to sit down, ensure that your

back is upright. Allow your arms to rest anywhere as long as you're comfortable.

2. Listen and connect with your body. Scan through your body while noticing your shape as you move from head to toe. Relax any points where you feel there is tension. Become curious about your body. Feel the sensations and the connection with the environment around you. Just breathe.

3. Now, listen to your breath. Just feel the natural flow of how you're breathing in and out. Don't change anything about how you're breathing. Just notice how beautiful it is to take in air and then let it out of your system. Pay attention to the places where you can feel your breath: your chest, your abdomen, your nostrils. Take one breath at a time as you try to connect with each breath.

4. In the process of listening to your body with all the silence around you, your mind might wander. There is a lot on your mind

and you cannot blame yourself if your mind is wandering, thinking about things not in the present moment. It's normal for this to happen. Even people who have meditated for years often find their minds wandering. So, don't be anxious because you cannot stop thinking about other things. Notice that your mind is wandering by whispering "wandering" or "thinking" inside your head. This raises your awareness of what is happening around you both physically and mentally. Gently shift your focus back to the breathing.

5. Maintain your focus for about 5-10 minutes. Ensure that you're noticing your breath. If your mind wanders again, bring it back to the point of focus without resisting any thoughts or sensations coming in.

6. Take a deep breath in as you conclude your exercise. Take a few moments to notice how you're feeling. Scan your body

to feel the positive changes that you have experienced. Continue relaxing for a few minutes while you allow your body to relax even more. Now appreciate yourself for finding time to practice this breathing exercise.

Other Breathing Techniques to Try

Besides the common breathing techniques that have been described above, there are other techniques that you can use to reduce stress or anxiety. Some of these exercises are engaging and you may find that you find it easy to practice them every day.

Lion's Breath

This is a dynamic breathing exercise that will help relieve tensions in your face and chest. Yoga enthusiasts often term this exercise as simhasana or simply, Lion's Pose (Cronkleton, 2019).

How to do it:

1. Find a comfortable and quiet place to sit. You can cross your legs or sit on your heels.

2. Spread your legs and press your palms against your knees. Spread your fingers wide while assuming this position.

3. Take a deep breath in through your nose while you open your eyes wide.

4. As you inhale, open your mouth wide. Allow your tongue to stick out and drop it to your chin.

5. Exhale through your mouth. As you do this, make a "ha" sound. This should be a long sound as though you were imitating a lion.

6. Repeat this exercise two or three times.

When should you practice the lion's breath? This breathing exercise is best suited for times when you're looking for energy to do something. Maybe you woke up feeling moody or tired. This breathing exercise can be a great way of achieving focus and avoiding procrastination.

4-7-8 Breathing

4-7-8 breathing is also termed as "relaxing breath." Just as the name suggests, this is a simple breathing technique that involves inhaling for 4 seconds, holding your breath for 7 seconds, and breathing out for 8 seconds.

One of the main advantages of this technique is that it helps to lower your anxiety levels. Similarly, this exercise can be performed when one is looking to catch some sleep after a long tiresome day. It might sound crazy but proponents argue that this breathing exercise can make you sleep in 1 minute (Fletcher, 2019).

There are several benefits that you can gain by practicing 4-7-8 breathing including, reducing anxiety, managing cravings, getting some sleep and controlling anger responses.

How to do it:

Before you start this exercise, find a comfortable position to take. Place the tip of your tongue on the roof of your mouth right behind your front teeth. After that, focus on the following pattern:

1. Start by emptying your lungs by breathing out.

2. Now breathe in slowly through your nose for 4 seconds.

3. Hold your breath for 7 seconds. Count this to 7.

4. After that, purse your lips and exhale stoutly through your mouth. Make a "whoosh" sound while you're at it for 8 seconds.

5. Repeat the process 4 times.

So, how often should you use this breathing technique? To start noticing the benefits in days, consider practicing this technique at least twice daily. After this exercise, you may feel lightheaded, especially if you're doing it for the very first time. As such, it's strongly recommended that you perform this exercise while lying or sitting down. This will prevent falls or dizziness.

The more you practice the 4-7-8 breathing technique, the sooner you will reap its benefits. You should remember to maintain the correct ratio as advised in the steps herein.

Breath Counting

Another common breathing technique is breath counting. It is an effective breathing exercise that can help you manage stress.

1. Sit comfortably on the floor or on a chair. Keep your head up and your back straight. Ensure that you're not assuming a stiff position. It's also important that you wear

something comfortable. No tight belt, shoes, bras.

2. Close your eyes and perform a body scan. Notice any tensions around your body. Scan from head to toe and let go of any tension that leaves you feeling stiff.

3. Relax and breathe. Using your diaphragm, take a deep breath in slowly through your nose. To ensure that you don't take in quick breaths, imagine having a small balloon under your belly button. Now, picture yourself inflating this balloon slowly with every breath you take.

4. With your breathing as your point of focus, for every breath you take in, count it as "one." Breathe out slowly. When you breathe in for the second time, count this as "two." Continue doing this to the count of five.

To prevent your mind from wandering, counting to five is recommended. If you continue counting past that, it is likely that you may think of other things, so it's good to keep it short for the best results.

Breathing exercises can help in gaining a calming effect since your heart rate will naturally slow down, helping you gain an opposite effect to the fight or flight response. When dealing with stress and anxiety, your breath can be a great tool to help you relax.

You may be wondering when is the best time for you to practice these breathing exercises? Breathing techniques can be performed at any time of the day. One breathing exercise can take less than five minutes. This means that you can practice breathing anytime you feel anxious or stressed. These exercises will help you relax. Instead of reacting to a situation, you will respond to it in the best way possible.

It's however recommended that you practice breathing exercises in the morning. Early morning is a special time of the day. If you live in a quiet neighborhood, you might notice the birds chirping welcoming the new day. Indeed, a new day is worth rejoicing. During this time, your mind is also booting up preparing itself for your daily routine. Starting your day on a high note has a profound impact on how you will approach your day. You will be energized since you started your day on a positive note. With your mind and body relaxed, you will approach everything from a more positive perspective. In the long run, this mentality will transform your life as you will value the importance of winning your day in the morning. Overall, don't forget to breathe when faced with a stressful situation or when your anxiety levels upsurge.

Chapter 6: Body Scan Techniques Guide

Stress and anxiety can leave you feeling tense with a lot of discomfort in your body. Sadly, our everyday stressors can be so overwhelming that you ignore the physical discomfort you may be experiencing. You're feeling pain on your shoulders or you're frequently experiencing headaches but you consider them to be normal after a tedious day. It's important to realize that the physical discomfort you're experiencing could be tied to your emotional state. Body scan meditation is a great way to relieve your body and mind of stress and anxiety. This practice doesn't just help you relax, but it aims to increase your awareness of your body from head to toe. Through your increased awareness, you can release tension from your body.

What is Body Scan Meditation?

Body scan practice is a type of meditation exercise that scans your body from head to toe. This technique is regarded as the most effective way to start mindfulness meditation. By scanning through your body from head to toe, you raise your awareness of every body part, relaxing areas of tension. During this meditation practice, your mind is brought to the present moment as you're more mindful of your body. Combining this benefit to the relaxation advantage that you gain makes this technique a powerful stress and anxiety reliever.

The goal of a body scan is to help you connect more with your body and reconnect with its physical aspect. You will be more aware of the sensations that you're feeling. Training your mind to stay in the present will be helpful in all facets of your life. You will be more accepting, you will learn to express gratitude for the things that happen in your life; overall, you will live mindfully and this will lead you to live a happy and fulfilling life.

Mastering the Practice of Body Scan

3-Minute Body Scan Meditation

To ensure that you find it easy to focus on your body scan meditation, we'll start with a short body scan practice. This scan can be performed while sitting, lying down or in any other posture, as long as you're comfortable.

1. Sit or lie down comfortably. Pay attention to your body as you start this scan.

2. Close your eyes if you find it difficult to focus.

3. Feel the weight of your body pressing on the floor or on the chair.

4. Take a long deep breath through your nose and exhale through your mouth.

5. Focus on how your body feels. Begin at the top of your head.

6. Continue scanning down your body as you notice any areas that are tense, stiff and uncomfortable.

7. Don't try to change anything. The point is to connect with your body and notice how every part feels.

8. Scan down your body, one section at a time until you reach your toes.

9. Notice the presence of your body and take a deep breath.

10. Breathe out through your pursed lips as you open your eyes.

This three-minute body scan can help bring you back to the present, especially when you feel that there is a lot going on in your mind. Don't allow yourself to ruminate as you can take advantage of this technique. You can manage stress and anxiety effectively if you develop a habit of being present.

10-Minute Body Scan Meditation

This body scan practice should take you about 10 minutes. Before you start this exercise, ensure that you have enough time to relax. Choose a comfortable and quiet place to perform this body scan.

1. Make yourself comfortable.
2. Close your eyes.
3. Bring awareness to your body by taking a deep breath in through your nose. Breathe out gently. Notice the position of your body in your space. Pay attention to how your body touches the floor or the seat

you're using. Take a few minutes to ensure that you connect deeply with your body.

4. When you're ready, take another deep breath. Notice how warm air is rushing through your nose into your lungs.

5. Gently shift your focus to your body. Start from the top of your head as you move from one section to another. One at a time. You could also start from your toes and move up towards your upper body. Pay attention to any sensations you may be feeling and let go. Proceed with the feet slowly and move up to your ankles, calves, etc. Continue focusing on the individual parts of your body without trying to change anything. You only need to become aware of how you feel and how your body feels.

6. Sensations in your body might vary from one end to the other. You may feel pressure in other parts, whereas you might feel cramps, cold, tightness, or a

tingling sensation in others. You may fail to feel these sensations and that you could feel that your body is just feeling neutral. Accept it. It's okay if this is what you're feeling. Go with the feeling that you're experiencing and continue scanning your body.

7. Strive to be curious about what's going on in your body. Make a deliberate effort to notice how each body part feels before moving to the next.

8. You may lose focus as you continue scanning your body. Observe how this is happening but don't make any judgments. Don't be frustrated that you cannot fully focus. It's normal for your mind to wander. Shift your focus back to your object of focus, your body. You can also bring your mind back to focus by paying attention to your breath. Try counting your breath as this will stop your mind from wandering.

9. When you feel that you've performed a full-body scan, open your eyes mindfully.

10. Don't be quick to get up and leave the room. Be mindful of how you're feeling and your surroundings. Notice how the room looks, look at the furniture, the walls, and anything around you. View these things as though you were noticing them for the first time. You're now relaxed. You're at peace with yourself. Now extend these good feelings to how you approach your day.

This 10-minute body scan can be done at any time of the day. However, it's highly recommended that you schedule in time for this exercise. Consider it a crucial meeting that you must have with yourself. You should realize that your day can get so packed that you might fail to remember to perform a body scan. In some cases, you might rush to do this practice while your mind is busy thinking of how you will resume working. Accordingly, it's very important to find an appropriate time to do a meditation body scan.

Powerful 20-Minute Body Scan Meditation

Start this exercise by making yourself comfortable. You can choose to lie on the floor or sit in a chair: make sure you feel comfortable so that you can achieve the focus that is required for this body scan meditation.

Find an environment that will not allow your mind to wander. It's crucial that you perform this body scan at a time when there is little or no interruption from your family members. Turn off any electronic devices that might distract you. Consider this time as your "me-time." A time for focusing on yourself. An opportunity to reconnect with your mind, body and soul, a special time for self-care: you shouldn't take it for granted.

It's important not to try and force things around. Don't push yourself to relax. Doing this will only create tension. The best way to relax is to accept everything that is happening around you. Become aware of each passing moment. Let go of wanting to fix things. We all have a tendency to try to change things that are happening around us. Avoid this by making sure that you allow things to be just as they are.

Follow these instructions while you take time to notice any activity of the mind and body. Treat yourself with kindness. Don't be too critical of your thoughts and let go of judgment. Just become aware and accept things as they are.

Keep in mind that there is no perfect way to feel while you're performing this body scan. There is nothing wrong with how you're feeling. It's okay to feel how you're feeling. So, there is no need to try and change it for you to feel right. Understand the importance of acceptance. Allow yourself to feel how you're feeling and realize that it's totally okay.

Now, gently close your eyes if you feel comfortable meditating with your eyes shut. Move on to sense the position of your body. Consider the chair or the mat that is supporting it off the ground.

Slowly bring your attention to your breath. Become aware of how you're breathing without trying to change anything. Just listen to your body breathe in and out. Notice how your body is moving as you inhale and exhale. As you inhale, notice how your chest is rising. And as you exhale, notice your chest falling. Follow the rhythm of your breath as you cherish how good it feels to breathe naturally and be alive.

With every breath that you take, your lungs are filled with warm air. As you breathe out, allow your body to rest even more. Your mind might become distracted. Notice when this is happening and bring your attention back to the point of focus; your breathing.

Now exhale deeply as you gently shift your focus to your body. Move down to your left foot and focus on the big toe. Pay attention to any sensations that you might be feeling here. Are you feeling cold or warm? Feel the touch of the socks or the stockings on your feet. Maybe you feel nothing. Just be there and notice what's going on. Move your attention from the big toe to the other toes of your left foot. Become mindful of the toenails and the skin. How do you feel between your toes?

Now shift your attention to the heel of your left foot. Notice the contact that it has with the mat or the floor. Gradually shift your focus to the top of the foot. Feel the change of skin and the surrounding temperature. Ensure that you notice all the sensations here, including the bones. Take a deep breath in. Just imagine yourself breathing through your left foot. Breathe in and out as if you could use your foot to breathe. As you breathe in, the fresh air will bring a sense of freshness in you. And as you breathe out, you release any tightness or tension on this part of the body. Just let go.

Moving up, bring your focus to your ankle. Become aware of the tendons, the bones and the skin. How does it feel? Take a deep breath of freshness into this part and breathe out to release any tension you might be feeling. Remember, you might not be feeling anything. It's okay to not feel anything. Understand this and move on to the next part of your body.

Bring your focus to your left leg just above your ankle. Feel its contact with the floor or the mat that is holding you above ground. Become aware of the shin bone, the calf muscle, and the skin around them. Pay attention to any sensations here. Take a deep breath in and out.

Explore the knee area. Focus on your left knee joint. Examine how you are feeling at the kneecap, the hinge, the cartilage, then move to the underside area. Are there any sensations here? Bring your attention to these sensations. Breathe in some freshness to this area then breathe out to release tension. Make sure that you're not judging any feelings that you may be experiencing. Be present with the feeling, release tension, and move on.

Move up to your left thigh. Feel the muscle of the leg here and the skin. You may focus more and feel how blood is circulating around this area. There could be some slight heaviness as the thighs carry a large muscle. Become aware of the thigh bone and notice how it sits in its socket.

Take a deep breath in as you allow some sense of freshness to fill your left leg from the bottom to the thigh area. Breathe out any form of tension that may be left out. Release any tiredness that you may be feeling. Relax.

Now bring your attention back to the thigh bone and make a smooth transition to the right hip. Move all the way to your right foot and start scanning your body from the big toe of this foot. How do you feel here? Be present here and do nothing to change how you're feeling.

Slowly shift your focus to the other toes. Notice how you're feeling around the toenails and the skin. How do you feel in between your toes? Become conscious of any sensations you may be experiencing while you make a deliberate effort to shift your attention to the ball of this foot.

Move to the arch of your right foot, then the heel. Pause for a moment here to notice how the skin of the heel is different. Afterward, move to the top part of the right foot. Feel the difference when focusing on the bones in this area. Now widen your focus to include the entire right foot. Take a deep breath of fresh air and breathe out tension or any form of tightness.

Bring your focus to your right ankle. Become aware of the skin, the bones, the tendons. Gradually move up to the right leg as you feel the pumping of blood around this area. Become aware of the skin, the calf muscle, the shin bone. Slowly draw your attention to the right knee. Examine this area for a few seconds connecting with any sensations that might be here.

As you continue feeling the pulsation of blood circulation in your system, slowly move with the flow to your right thigh. Explore the feeling of the muscle and of the thigh bone. Breathe in some freshness into this area of your body. Breathe out to release toxins and congestion. Relax.

Now bring your focus to the middle area of your body, the pelvic bowl. Pay attention to your hip bones. Become aware of the organs located around this part of the body. The bladder, the reproductive organs, and the intestines. Notice how your buttocks are providing you with the support off the ground. How are you feeling around this area? Maybe you're feeling heavy or light, or perhaps you're feeling some tightness.

Move your attention up from the lower back to the spine. Pay attention to every inch of your spine as you notice how each vertebra feels. Become aware of your back muscles, your skin, and any sensations around this area. Allow your back muscles to relax with every breath you take in.

Gently bring your focus to the middle area of your back where your kidneys sit. Pay attention to the rib cage area. Become mindful of the expansion and contraction of the rib cage as you breathe in and out. Notice where the rib cage connects with the spine, at the back of your lungs, the back of your heart or near the shoulder blades. While doing this, move further up to the area where the spine connects with the skull.

Take a deep breath in to expand your entire back area. Allow freshness to fill this area and let go of any tension. Breathe out and allow your back to rest more into the floor or the chair that you're seated on.

Bring your attention to your chest. Continue feeling the expanding and contracting of the rib cage as you inhale and exhale. Focus on how the rib cage is also moving from the sides under your armpits. Become aware of how the heart is cushioned between the lungs. As you do this, notice how the lungs and the heart are working together to help you breathe in oxygen and breathe out carbon dioxide.

Now slowly draw your awareness to your chest muscles and the breasts. Notice how the skin feels here. Take a deep breath in, bringing in rejuvenated energy within you. Fill your lungs with new energy and breathe out releasing any tightness inside you. What are some of the emotions that you feel around this area? You may or may not feel anything. Don't push yourself to change anything if you're not feeling anything. Similarly, if there are emotions that come and go, just notice them and move on. Stay aware, and not judgmental.

Move on to your arms. Start by focusing on your fingertips. Become aware of the sensation at the top of your fingertips. Perhaps you feel some dryness or moisture? How about the skin, the fingernails, the knuckles, the joints, the palms? How do you feel around this area? Breathe in some freshness to this area of your body and breathe out releasing any tightness or tension you may be feeling.

Continue with the scan raising your awareness to your upper arm, your shoulders, your throat, the back of the head, and your cheeks. It's important that you pay attention to all sensations that you may be feeling around these areas. While scanning through these areas, ensure that you maintain your neutral mindset. For every deep breath you take, consider this as your way of breathing in fresh energy into the part of your body that you're focusing on. When you breathe out, you release tension and toxins from your body.

As you approach the end of this 20-minute body scan, let go of any control that you may have. Allow yourself to be still, inhaling and exhaling freely as you notice your surroundings. Your acceptance to how things are is a form of healing that is gained through body scan meditation. As such, it's important to accept your world as it is without trying to change it.

Take a third-eye perspective and see yourself as a complete being, worthy of living the best life you can. See the fullness of your ability to live and love those who are around you. Realize that you're now fully awake and relaxed. Don't be in a rush to get up and leave the room. Take a few moments to bring your attention to your body. Notice the good feeling that flows in you at this point. Stretch gently. When you're ready, congratulate yourself for taking the time to focus on yourself. Resume your activities building on the good feeling that you gained through this relaxation technique.

Chapter 7: Progressive Relaxation Techniques Guide

Progressive muscle relaxation (PMR) is an effective relaxation technique that is often used to manage stress and anxiety. It can also help in relieving insomnia as well as symptoms of chronic pain. The basic idea behind this form of relaxation is that it involves tightening or tensing of muscles, one area at a time followed by relaxation of these muscles to release tension. When faced with stress and anxiety, it's common to feel that your muscles are tensed almost throughout the day. Practicing PMR will help you notice that there is a huge difference between tensed and relaxed muscles. Some medical experts use PMR alongside cognitive behavioral therapy techniques. However, this doesn't mean that using PMR alone is not effective. Once you master this relaxation technique, you will have a greater sense of control over how your body responds to stress and anxiety.

Preparing for Relaxation

Preparing for any relaxation technique demands that you should set aside some time to complete the exercise without any distractions. This applies when you're about to practice progressive muscle relaxation. The exercise will take about 15 minutes. Ensure that you find a quiet and peaceful place to practice PMR.

During the first few days, it's vital that you practice this technique at least twice a day. This guarantees that you master the relaxation technique as soon as possible. Remember, the faster you get the hang of it, the better. You will effectively manage your anxiety and stress. Ideally, you will approach each day full of energy and optimism. This is something that people who are anxious or stressed find impossible to accomplish.

There are a few concerns that you should bear in mind while practicing PMR. Do you suffer from any physical injuries? If you have a history of physical injuries that might lead to muscle pain or cramps, then it's crucial that you talk to your doctor about the exercises that you would be performing.

It's also vital that you select ideal surroundings to practice this technique. Minimize or prevent any distractions to your five senses. Start by turning off the TV, radio, and any electrical appliances that might distract you. Adjust your lighting to soft if possible as this will provide you with a suitable environment to concentrate.

Comfort is key to successful progressive muscle relaxation. Find a chair that makes you comfortable. Your back should be upright and your head should be well supported. Wear loose clothing to avoid any discomfort. If possible, consider taking off your shoes.

You must practice PMR while your mind and body are calm and fresh. Your ability to focus might be affected after eating a heavy meal. Accordingly, it's recommended not to practice after a big meal. The same case applies to intoxicants, like alcohol. You should realize that you cannot accurately focus with an intoxicated mind. So, make sure you do it with a fresh mind.

Instructions

Muscle tension is often associated with anxiety, stress, and panic attacks. This is the natural way in which our bodies respond to potentially dangerous situations. Some of these situations might not be life-threatening, but our bodies generally react in the same way. This is what we talked about at the beginning of this manual. It's the fight-or-flight response.

Unfortunately, a good number of people are not aware of the muscle groups which are tensed in their bodies. PMR can help you focus on different muscle groups and relax the areas where you feel tense. Just as the name suggests, progressive muscle relaxation involves a step-by-step analysis of muscle groups. So, the key issue is to move from one specific muscle group at a time. First, you feel the tension in that muscle, and then you release the tension. This is done from head to toe scanning throughout your body. With the PMR technique, you will learn to recognize specific muscle groups and to differentiate between tensed sensations and feelings of deep relaxation.

You can practice PMR while sitting on a chair or lying down. Particular muscle groups are tensed for 5-7 seconds, released and then relaxed for 20-30 seconds. The length of time can vary; you don't have to adhere to the time mentioned here strictly. It's, however, strongly recommended that you stick to the indicated time when you're practicing PMR during the first few days. This practice should be repeated at least twice daily. Of course, some muscles are harder to relax. When this happens, focus on that particular muscle tensing and releasing it for about five times.

You might be distracted during the first few attempts. Once you memorize the steps that should be followed, you can easily close your eyes and focus on one muscle group at a time.

To help you understand the practice better, the progressive muscle relaxation instructions are divided into two parts. The first section features the basic procedure. You can memorize this section and recall it while you're practicing PMR. This makes it easy for you to familiarize yourself with the different muscle groups in your body. Take frequent pauses where necessary.

The second section is shorter than the first as it focuses on tensing and relaxing several muscle groups at a time. This means that you will spend less time doing the relaxation practice.

Levels of Tensing

There are three levels of tensing you can incorporate in your PMR practice. Once you're conversant with the forms of tensing, you can settle for one that serves you best.

Active Tensing

Essentially, this level of tensing involves the simple process of actively relaxing a specific muscle group at a time. You should tense these muscle groups as tightly as you can without harming yourself. While doing this, pay attention to the resulting sensations after tensing your muscles, then relax that part of the muscle and examine how you feel. During the tension phase, it's recommended that you breathe diaphragmatically.

Tensing your muscle groups as tightly as you can help in raising your awareness about areas of your body where you often carry chronic tension. People with no history of injuries should use this form of tensing. Picture yourself carrying a heavy box for an extended period. How do you feel when you drop this box? You will feel good and relaxed, right? This is how active tensing makes you feel.

Threshold Tensing

Threshold tensing is similar to active tensing but different in the sense that you should only tense your muscles slightly. This form of tensing is ideal for areas that are very tense or injured. It's effective once you get the idea of how the basic form of active tensing works. If you have a history of injuries or chronic pain, threshold tensing comes highly recommended.

Passive Tensing

Passive tensing is where you simply notice tension in specific muscle groups. Instead of tensing your muscle groups as advised in active or threshold tensing, here you only notice areas of your body that are tensed. This type of tensing is best used when you're not feeling any tension in your body. However, all these forms of tensing are useful in helping you achieve a deepened state of relaxation.

Basic Procedure

Find a comfortable position to assume. You can either sit or lie down as long as you're comfortable. Choose a quiet room where you will not be interrupted.

Make a deliberate effort to focus on your body. Your mind might start to wonder. Notice this happening but gently bring your mind back to your object of focus, the muscles you're tensing.

Breathe in diaphragmatically through your abdomen. Pause and hold your breath for 5 seconds. Now breathe out slowly through your pursed lips. While you're breathing in and out, notice the movement of your chest and your stomach. This helps your mind to stay focused and in the present moment.

As you breathe out, imagine tension being released out of your body. For every breath you take, you breathe in some fresh air that brings in relaxation to tense muscles in your body. Breathe in... and out. Feel your body already relaxing.

From this moment onwards, remember to keep breathing and allow your body to relax completely.

Now let's begin.

Start by tightening the muscles in your forehead. To do this, raise your eyebrows as high as you can. Don't strain too much. Just put in extra effort to raise your eyebrows up. Hold your eyebrows in that position for five seconds. Release them abruptly as you allow yourself to feel that tension drop.

Pause for roughly 10 seconds.

Now tense your mouth and cheeks by smiling widely. Hold for 5 roughly seconds and release. Recognize how your face feels soft.

Pause for roughly 10 seconds.

After that, move on to tense your eye muscles. Shut your eyelids as tightly as you can. Hold for roughly 5 seconds and release.

Pause for roughly 10 seconds.

Slowly pull your head to look up as though you were gazing at the ceiling. Maintain this position for about 5 seconds, then release. Feel the tension melting away from your neck muscles.

Pause for roughly 10 seconds.

Take a moment to appreciate the relaxed feeling of your head and neck.

Take a deep breath in... and breathe out.

Breathe in again, and out.

Let go of all the stress and anxiety that you might be feeling.

Breathe in and out.

Move on to clench your fists tightly without struggling too much. Hold for roughly 5 seconds. Make it count. Release.

Pause for roughly 10 seconds.

Time to flex your biceps. Tightly flex your biceps as you feel the tension building up around this muscle. Visualize your biceps tightening. Maintain this position for about 5 seconds. Release.

Take a deep breath in, and breathe out.

Next, tighten your tricep muscles. Extend your arms out and tightly lock elbows. Hold this position for about 5 seconds. Release.

Take a long deep pause for about 10 seconds. Relax.

Raise your shoulders up high as though they could touch your ears. Maintain the position for about 5 seconds. Release. Feel the heaviness of your shoulders as they drop back to their original position.

Take a long deep pause for about 10 seconds. Relax.

Now, tense your upper back. Pull your shoulders back as if you were trying to make the shoulder blades touch. Hold that position for about 5 seconds. Relax.

Take a long deep pause for about 10 seconds. Relax.

Tense your chest. Take a deep breath in... Pause for 5 seconds. Breathe out. Let go of all the tension in this area.

Gently move to your lower body and tighten your stomach muscles. Suck them in. Maintain this position for about 5 seconds. Relax.

Take a long deep pause for about 10 seconds. Relax.

Slowly arch your lower back. Hold this position for about 5 seconds. Release.

Take a long deep pause for about 10 seconds. Relax.

Pause for a moment to appreciate the sagginess of your upper body. Let go of all the tension and stress inside.

Next, tighten your buttocks. Maintain this position for 5 seconds. Relax.

Take a long deep pause for about 10 seconds. Relax.

Now, tense your thighs by pressing your knees together. Imagine holding a penny between your knees. Maintain this position for 5 seconds. Relax.

Take a long deep pause for about 10 seconds. Relax.

Tense your feet by curling your toes. Hold this position for about 5 seconds. Relax.

Take a long deep pause for about 10 seconds. Relax.

Perform a quick body scan as you acknowledge the wave of relaxation throughout your body from head to toe. Feel the lightness within you.

Breathe in... pause... breathe out.

Breathe in... pause... breathe out.

Shorter PMR Technique

Once you've mastered the PMR technique, you can quickly relax your muscles without necessarily going through all the basic procedures. This is achieved by tensing several muscle groups at a time and relaxing them. It's important that you remember to compare how your muscles feel when tense. and when relaxed. By distinguishing between relaxed and tense muscles, you will value the importance of relaxation in your body.

Let's begin. Tightly curl your fists and tense your forearms and biceps. Hold this position for about 5 seconds. Relax.

Pull your head backward as though you're gazing at the ceiling. Roll it clockwise to make a complete circle. Perform the same process anticlockwise. Relax.

Now tense your face muscles. Smile widely as you feel your cheeks tighten, Wrinkle your forehead and squint your eyes while you hunch your shoulders. Maintain this position for about 5 seconds. Relax.

Arch your shoulders back so that your shoulder blades can meet. Take a deep breath into your chest as you tighten your stomach muscles to hold this breath. Hold for about 5 seconds. Relax.

Curl your toes, tighten your thighs, calves and buttocks. Hold this position for 5 seconds. Relax.

Summary of the Muscle Groups to Tense

The following is a list of the muscle groups that you should focus on tensing while doing progressive muscle relaxation.

Muscle Group	What to Do
Forehead	Raise your eyebrows high and hold.
Bridge of the nose	Frown as much as you can.
Cheeks and jaws	Smile widely.
Eye muscles	Squint your eyelids tightly.
Neck muscles	Pull your head back as though you're looking at the ceiling.
Hands	Clench your fists.
Biceps	Tighten or flex your biceps.
Triceps	Extend your arms out and lock your elbows.
Shoulders	Lift your shoulders as if you want them to touch your ears.
Upper back	Pull your shoulders back tightly.

Chest	Take a deep breath in and hold.
Stomach muscles (Abs)	Suck your stomach muscles in.
Lower back	Arch your lower back.
Buttocks	Tighten.
Thighs	Press your knees together.
Feet	Pull your toes towards you.
Calves	Tighten your calves.
Toes	Curl your toes.

Chapter 8: Physical Meditation Techniques Guide

This section will take you through physical meditation practices as a technique that will help you relax and master calming your mind.

Meditation is a term that has been inaccurately and loosely used in the modern-day world. As a result, there is so much confusion about how to practice meditation every day. Some folks use the term meditation to refer to the everyday practice of thinking. Others misunderstand it as fantasizing or daydreaming. Meditation (Dhyana) is not anything close to these definitions.

What is Meditation?

Simply put, meditation refers to the technique of resting the mind and attaining a higher state of consciousness. Meditation is not a religion. Rather, it is a science. As such, it is a practice that sticks to a specific order and that its results can be verified (Rama, n.d.). When practicing meditation, the mind is clear and relaxed. It is inwardly focused to help in fathoming a deepened state of ourselves. During the process of meditating, you're wide awake and alert.

Nonetheless, the mind is not focused on the external world or anything that is happening around you. Instead, it focuses on your calm inner state, and this helps to quieten the mind. Once this state is achieved, nothing can distract you, and meditation deepens further.

Turning Inward

One interesting thing that you've always been taught in life is to focus on the external world. However, no school has taught us how to focus on our inner selves. The issue here is that we forget who we are and we become strangers to ourselves. The absence of self-understanding affects our lives in many ways. It is one of the main reasons why we are often disappointed in life and why most of the relationships we enter into fail to work.

Our education systems cultivate a small portion of the mind and the vast realm of unconsciousness remains undisciplined and unknown. Perhaps you might have heard that the entire body is in the mind, but the entire mind is not in the body. This phrase is true, bearing in mind that the better part of the mind remains unexploited. It is through the practice of meditation that the mind can be truly developed and controlled.

So, what is the goal of meditation? Meditation seeks to go beyond the mind and connect with our very nature - which is characterized by happiness, peace and bliss. People who meditate more often have a deeper understanding that the mind stands between ourselves and the understanding of our essential nature. It can be argued that the mind has a mind of its own, which is unruly and undisciplined. The mind will rebel against any attempts to tune it to follow a certain path. Accordingly, most people who meditate experience daydreams or fantasies. Very few people achieve the stillness that is obtained through genuine deep meditation.

Oftentimes we are taught how to adjust to the external world. We are never taught how to calm our minds and examine ourselves from within. This is what you learn through meditation. By learning how to be still and look within yourself, you gain the highest form of happiness that can be achieved by a human being. You ought to realize that all other external forms of joys are momentary. The joy of meditation is everlasting. Well, you might think that we are exaggerating things here. But it's the plain truth. The benefits of meditation are true, and they are supported by a long line of philosophers who attained the truth behind it.

You also stand to benefit from meditation, as this guide will take you through some basics of meditation. In reality, you may not become a pro from the word go. However, practice makes perfect. The more you practice how to meditate, the more you achieve a higher state of stillness that deepens your meditation practice. It's all about your commitment to the practice. Don't jump into it with excitement expecting quick results within a day. Make it a habit and you will certainly see a transformation in your life.

Guide to Cultivating Stillness

The basic idea behind meditation is that you should learn how to be still. For you to learn how to be still, you have to begin with your body before you progress to your thoughts. Traditionally, yoga required that one should be guided by a teacher to achieve the right meditation posture termed as "asana." Today, this is something that you can practice at home. By meditating regularly, you can master the art and you will find it easy to achieve the right posture to meditate.

Let's begin.

Find an uncluttered room that is quiet and where you will not be disturbed while meditating. Make yourself comfortable. Sit on a chair or the floor cushioned by a mat. Keep your back straight and gently close your eyes.

Now bring your attention to your body. Become aware of your whole body from head to toe. Relax. Release all the tension that you're feeling in your body. Let go. Meditation is all about letting go. First, let go of physical tension before you progress to your thoughts.

With your body relaxed and calm, bring your attention to your breath. Notice the areas of the body that are used as you breathe. It's important that you breathe diaphragmatically as this will help you achieve a higher state of relaxation. Continue focusing on your breath. Just notice how air is moving in and out of your body without trying to control it. You may notice that the first few moments your breath is irregular. Gradually, it gets smooth.

Your object of focus is your breath. Continue focusing on your breath in an accepting way. Don't judge, just be there to experience the beauty of breathing in and out. Open yourself fully until you feel like there is no difference between you and your breathing.

Plenty of thoughts will come to mind. You may think, "Am I doing this in the correct way?" Or "When will this end?" Or "Maybe I should have closed the door!" Or "My neck hurts." It's okay for your mind to wander. Each thought that comes to mind will require some form of response from you, either an action, judgment, or a general interest in trailing the thought further. You may also want to lose the thought.

As you continue meditating, realize that you're only required to raise your awareness. So, become aware of how your mind is restless. Notice the thoughts that come and go without taking any action or being judgmental. You only need to be aware and let go.

Paying Attention

The science of meditation is all about attending. For instance, if you're focusing on your breath and a certain thought came to mind, you should attend to it. The point here is that you should be present to notice this thought. Accept it and it will pass. After that, you should bring your attention to your object of focus.

Usually, we tend to react to our thoughts and this is what keeps your mind busy day and night. At times you're left in a sea of confusion not knowing what to do. Meditation practice helps you to attend to whatever is happening within you without reacting. This is where all the difference comes about. Through regular meditation, you can stop your mind from incessant wandering. It is from this freedom that you will realize who you are. You will begin to realize that you're not your mind, and you will live a life full of joy and contentment.

With time, you will value the deep state of relaxation and relief that you gain from meditation. Ideally, you will have given yourself an inner vacation - an experience of a lifetime that you may have never enjoyed before.

Ordinarily, people react to experiences that come to them in the same way they react to their thoughts. For instance, if relationships do not work, people become upset. If they lose money, they become frustrated. When something negative is said about you, you become depressed. All these prove one thing: your moods/feelings are dictated by what comes before you. For that reason, you may feel as though your life is a vicious cycle of bad experiences. The problem is that you react even moments before you fully experience what you're reacting to. This is as a result of the interpretations that you have in mind about what might happen.

Your fears, resistances and prejudices limit you from enjoying life as it is. The control that you gain from meditation will help you attend to what is taking place in the present moment. Instead of reacting to things, you will understand that you're not your mind. Through acceptance, you will learn how to take on ideal responses that are most helpful to your everyday circumstances.

What Are the Signs of Progress?

You may be concerned about how you will know that you're making progress. The important thing to keep in mind is that you need to practice meditating more often for you to experience the benefits of it. Obviously, you don't plant a seed today to reap the fruits the following day. It takes time. Be gentle and patient with yourself, and practice consistently.

Top 5 Yoga Poses to Help You Relax

Statistics from the National Institute of Health shows that 9.5% of Americans do yoga exercises. As more and more people begin practicing yoga, studies reveal that many physical and mental benefits are gained by those who practice yoga. Yoga is a Sanskrit term which means the "union of the body and mind" (Tarantola, 2018). Some of the physical benefits gained from yoga include increased strength and flexibility, toning muscles, lowering blood pressure, and most importantly, encouraging relaxation. There are studies that show that yoga can also be used to alleviate back pain and arthritis, in addition to boosting mental and heart health (Tarantola, 2018).

The following are five of the best yoga poses that you can use to relax your body and mind.

Legs Up the Wall

Legs up the wall is a popular yoga pose simply because you don't have to strain yourself to assume this pose. The best part is that it can be done anywhere. It's the perfect way to unwind after a stressful day.

Find some space around you where you can lie down with your head facing away from the wall. Lift your legs up so that they can rest on the wall. For additional support, consider placing a pillow under your hips. Ensure that you're comfortable in this position for optimal relaxation benefits. You can play some soothing music to help you deepen your relaxation. Take this moment to allow your mind and body to relax. Learn to let go of any tension, thoughts, or worries may be holding on to. Make an effort to bring your mind to the present moment to achieve the calmness that you need.

Child's Pose

This is a wonderful pose that will help you relieve tension around the hips and the lower back. Start this pose by assuming a tabletop position. Slowly bring your big toes inward towards one another and widen your knees. Gently push your hips back so that your haunches are close to your heels. Now walk your hands in front of you and gradually lower your chest to the floor. Let go and relax your whole body. For extra support, consider putting a pillow under your belly. Once you've achieved the right posture, follow your breathing exercise as you release any tension from your body. Maintain this position for about 10 deep breaths. If possible, add props to modify the pose for maximum relaxation.

Forward Bend/Fold

Forward bend/fold can be done while sitting or standing. Both postures will provide you with plenty of relaxation benefits. Before assuming this position, start by taking deep breaths in and out. Do this until you notice your breath is smooth. If you want to perform this exercise while sitting down, get yourself comfortable with your legs stretched out. Next, walk your hands towards your heels as much as you can. Don't worry about touching your heels. Simply ensure that you stretch your back without straining. Lower your chest to your knees. Relax your neck and head and face forward.

If you are performing this exercise while standing, stand upright and fold yourself from this position. Move your arms to the back of your feet. Maintain this posture for 10 deep breaths.

This pose helps stimulate vital organs such as the kidneys and liver. It also improves digestion while stretching out the hamstrings, calves, and hips. Additionally, it can lower your stress levels thanks to the calming effect it has on your mind.

Corpse Pose

You might think that this is perhaps the easiest pose to assume. Well, you're wrong. Yogis argue that this is a challenging pose as most people struggle to lie there and just relax. You may notice that this pose is commonly used at the end of a yoga class. Generally, it helps to relax and calm the mind. Other potential benefits include reducing headaches, fatigue, and helping with insomnia.

Tree Pose

This is yet another awesome yoga pose for beginners. It helps to ensure that you achieve focus and clarity while standing on one foot. To practice this posture, begin by standing on both feet. After that, place your left foot on your inner right upper thigh. Put your hands together in a prayer position. Find an object in front of you to focus on, for example, you can use a candle as your object of focus.

Maintain the position for 10 breaths and switch sides. While in this position, ensure that you avoid leaning on the standing leg. It's also helpful to keep your abdominals engaged in the process.

Other Physical Meditation Techniques: Qigong

Qigong, often pronounced *chee-gun*, refers to an ancient Chinese healing exercise and technique that involves controlled breathing meditation and movement exercises (Palermo, 2015). Practicing qigong helps to ensure you maintain your Jing, bolster, and balance your Qi energy while at the same time enlightening your Shen (spirit/mind). The term "Jing" refers to your spirit (Campbell, n.d.). Qigong helps to maintain and balance your gentle spirit. Your "Qi" is your life energy, the energy that flows in all living things ("What Is Qi Energy?," n.d.)

Just like yoga, there are numerous types of qigong practiced all over the world. Some of these exercises take the form of meditation and breathing exercises to enhance spirituality and health. Others are more vivacious and they include martial arts.

Qigong and Tai Chi

Most people tend to think that qigong and tai chi are similar. However, based on the definition of both practices, they are very far from it. Tai chi, also known as tai chi chuan, is a self-paced technique of stretching and other physical exercises (Tai chi: A gentle way to fight stress, 2018). Each posture used in tai chi flows into the next posture without taking breaks. The goal is to see your body in constant motion. It's for this reason that tai chi is sometimes referred to as moving meditation. Practicing tai chi regularly has numerous health benefits for the mind, body, and spirit.

Qigong, on the other hand, is usually identified as the internal part of tai chi. Qigong exercises involve stationary movements repeated several times. "Qi" is the energy that flows in us and makes us feel alive. It's through this energy that people experience different types of emotions.

The striking difference between qigong and tai chi is that the latter involves movements that are often practiced for a specific situation. Tai chi involves full-body movements that flow in a sequence. Concepts and theories can be used in tai chi classes. Some movements of qigong can also be used in these classes, but qigong practice does not have to include tai chi.

To clearly distinguish between the two, think of a bodybuilder who strives to make their biceps bigger. In this case, the bodybuilder will build this muscle using repeated bicep curls exercises To effectively build this muscle, the bodybuilder will have to focus on that muscle only. Likewise, qigong focuses on one particular issue that one might be suffering from either physically, emotionally or spiritually. Tai chi, on the contrary, is like taking care of the whole body by exercising regularly.

You may be wondering whether you have to be physically fit for you to practice qigong or tai chi. The truth is that you don't have to be in great shape to practice either of these ancient meditation exercises. The aim of these meditation techniques is to bolster your strength, flexibility and balance.

The exciting thing about these forms of exercise is that they can be practiced anywhere and you don't require any equipment to start. When practiced correctly, tai chi and qigong can be ideal approaches to improve your overall health.

Chapter 9: Visualization Techniques Guide

Visualization, also termed as guided imagery, is a relaxation technique that uses the power of imagination to evoke positive emotions. This technique works in a simple way. You only need to picture yourself in a relaxed scene and live in the moment. It might sound too simple or too silly, but rest assured that it works. The basic idea behind visualization involves the notion of coming up with a detailed mental image of a peaceful and relaxing environment. This relaxation technique can be practiced on its own, but you can also incorporate it alongside the physical relaxation practices that we have discussed in this manual, like progressive muscle relaxation.

Why Visualization Works

You may be wondering whether visualization can really help relieve you of stress and anxiety. Guided imagery will help you relax due to a number of reasons. This technique involves a crucial element of distraction that redirects your attention away from something that might be stressing you and draws your focus towards something else. Consider visualization as a non-verbal instruction to the unconscious mind and body to act as though it was in a relaxed and calm state.

Visualization also works by bringing back good relaxation memories that will evoke pleasant sensations, which will eventually help you relax. Just like other forms of guided meditation, the goal of visualization is to help you learn how to disconnect yourself from moment to moment fixation, which often contributes to increased levels of stress and anxiety. Instead, you learn to detach yourself from thoughts and feelings and just notice them streaming through your mind and body. Practicing visualization guarantees that you improve on how you respond to stressful situations.

Here is a brief practice that you can try to have an idea of how the visualization technique works.

Think of a food that you love to eat. Really, stop for a moment and think about it. Bring the picture in mind. Close your eyes and imagine the food you thought about in front of you. Notice how amazing the food looks. Imagine its aroma and taste. Picture yourself in the present moment having the food you're thinking about.

After the brief exercise, if you were somewhat hungry, then hunger pangs must have started striking you. Perhaps your mouth is watering at the thought of the food. This example should show you the strong connection that your thoughts have with your body. Visualization leverages on this phenomenon to change how you feel.

Another example that can help you understand how visualization actually works is the effect that films can have on your emotional state. Have you ever felt depressed after watching a heartbreaking movie? Maybe the movie even left you shedding tears. This is how your thoughts can influence your moods. By mastering the power of visualization, you can use it to your advantage to influence your emotional state as you desire.

Visualization Techniques for Anxiety and Stress Reduction

The following visualization techniques should help you manage your stress and anxiety. It's strongly recommended that you use these techniques at a specified time set aside to visualize every day.

Creative Visualization of a Favorable Outcome

This type of visualization involves the idea of creating a particular outcome that you want out of a certain situation. This technique is best used when faced with a stressful situation. In this case, you should picture yourself at a time when you've solved the issue that you might be facing.

How to do it

Find a quiet place where you can make yourself comfortable. Gently close your eyes and take a deep breath. Bring your attention to the issue that is stressing you. Maybe finances have been an issue and your mind hasn't settled as a result. It could be that your marriage is not okay and it has been stressing you. Don't associate yourself with the stressful issue you may be experiencing. The key issue is to visualize the issue so that you can visualize the other side of the stressful scenario.

Now, with the issue in mind, picture yourself feeling okay after you've resolved the problem you have been facing. Imagine yourself feeling peaceful, calm, and happy that the issue has totally been resolved. Don't worry about how the matter was resolved. Visualization doesn't focus on the solutions. Rather, it creates an image that is opposite to the negative feeling that you may be experiencing. Visualization takes your mind to a beautiful life full of joy, happiness and calmness.

It's crucial that you envisage every little detail relating to the issue you wish to resolve. What does your immediate environment look like? What are you wearing? Who are you communicating with? Remain in the visualized room and notice anything tangible. What do you see? These tangible items are helpful as they strengthen your visualization.

Most people who have successfully used visualization to manage stress agree that this exercise is effective as it brings solutions to the forefront. How does this happen? In the process of visualizing that your problem has been resolved, chances are that practical solutions to your issue might come to mind. The advantage gained here is that this lowers or expels the likelihood of feeling stressed.

Visualization as Diversion from Stress

This visualization technique can be used when you're feeling extremely stressed. The basic idea behind this technique is to imagine a peaceful scene as a means of momentary relief. The scene here can be something that you strongly desire. Visualize being in a deserted beach that you've always imagined yourself visiting, or playing with a kitten. Visualize anything that makes you relaxed and happy, and be in that moment.

How to do it

Make yourself comfortable in a quiet surrounding. Empty your mind and take a few deep breaths in and out. Now create a picture of something that would make you feel calm, relaxed, and happy.

Again, visualize all the little details that relate to the relaxation scenario that you have in mind. If you're thinking about a place, what time is it there? Is it night time or day time? Do you notice the sun shining on a body of water next to you? What are some of the sounds that you hear? What are people talking about in this beautiful place?

If you're thinking about playing with your lovely pet, what color is it? Does it have a name? What game are you playing with the pet?

The more detailed your visualization is, the better the technique will work. It draws your attention away from the mental clutter that contributed to increased stress and anxiety. This form of visualization is best used when stress mounts up or when you feel you're overly anxious. It takes practice for you to find it easy to virtually visit that beautiful place in your mind where you can relax. The good thing about this visualization exercise is that it can be practiced at any time of the day. Regardless, it makes a lot of sense for you to set some time aside to use this technique to relax and calm your mind. Remember, it's by achieving a peaceful state of mind that you'll be able to see your productivity increase and feel good about yourself and the life you live.

Visualization With Deep Breathing

Deep breathing is a powerful relaxation technique that we explored in chapter 5. Combining this technique with visualization promises outstanding results. When these techniques work together, both the mind and the body are brought to a deepened state of relaxation.

How to do it

It's recommended that you lie down to practice this technique. Start by taking a deep breath in and out. Use your breath as your object of focus. Listen to your body as you breathe in cool, fresh air into your body. Feel the warmth of the air as it escapes through your nostrils releasing tension from within.

Next, become aware of your body. Notice your body lying down and the posture that you've assumed. Feel the contact between your body and the floor. Scan your body from the top of your head all the way down to your toes. Pay attention to all the sensations that come and go as you explore your body.

Now visualize all kinds of stress leaving your system in the form of waves through each breath. Widen your visualization. What do these waves look like? Are they colored? If so, what color are they? Which part of the body is discharging the most waves of stress?

Just like other forms of visualization, the more detailed your imagery is, the more effective your practice will be. This is a good opportunity for you to leverage your creativity and create a peaceful world in your mind where you can relax and calm your mind.

Happy Memory Visualization

There is no denying the fact that happy memories have a remarkable effect on our emotional state. Visualizing yourself being happy at a certain time is somewhat distinct from visualizations of physical things like money or your dream home. This type of visualization is highly effective as it manifests true happiness in your life. The best part is that once you learn to take your mind to these beautiful moments, you can also do the same in stressful situations.

When you're not feeling satisfied with your circumstances or with yourself, you can switch your mind to happy memories that fuel you with joy and laughter. Happy feelings will always be a useful tool to help you live a fulfilling life as these emotions strengthen the power of your thoughts. Any negative feelings that might have been hiding in your subconscious mind will automatically be eliminated. This void will be filled with positive and productive thoughts that can lead you to live a better life.

How to do it

Start by having a specific goal in mind. What do you want to achieve from this visualization? Of course, you want to imagine yourself being happy.

Select an image that is personal to you and brings back happy memories in your life. Don't be in a rush to pick an image. Take a few minutes to listen to your thoughts as you choose a memory of something that makes you truly happy. We all have that one moment that we can relate to. A time when we were genuinely happy. Choose that memory and use it for this visualization.

One thing that you should remember from the previous chapters is that practicing relaxation exercises every day is the best way of ensuring you master these techniques. Likewise, schedule your time to practice self-care through visualization. With time, your visualization will gain more clarity and you will start seeing manifestations in your life.

Let's begin.

Take a deep breath in and out. Relax and clear your mind. Pay attention to your breathing as it helps in clearing the mental jumble that is preventing you from relaxing.

Now bring your happy memory in sight. What were you wearing when this memorable occasion occurred? Who were you with? What did your friend or partner wear for the occasion? What color of clothes did you wear? Include all the fine details to strengthen your visualization.

You may fail to remember all the details, but make sure that you fill these gaps with anything that comes to mind. The important thing is to have a clear picture of this memory.

Visualize everything in your happy memory through all your five senses. Think about what you can touch, see, hear, smell or even taste. Maybe you had a wonderful meal that day. Bring your attention to all the senses to strengthen the visualized picture.

Next, take a third-person perspective of the happy scenario. Play this scene as though you were watching a movie. What was it that you did? Who were you with? What did they say or do that made you happy? Give yourself enough time to play this scene to bring back the good feelings that you felt during that day. It's all in your brain.

After that, take a first-person view of everything that happened. It's all about you and how you felt. Let the good feelings flow within you from all corners of your body. Savor the precious moment and stay there for a few minutes.

Continue playing this happy memory as you allow yourself to enjoy the experience through all your five senses. You're happy and peaceful as you can clearly remember and relate to.

Now wrap it up. You've achieved your goal of visualization. Gently let go of the image and approach the rest of the day with the renewed sense of happiness that you just felt.

Visualization for Self-Motivation

Stress can take a considerable toll on your life. It can quickly extinguish any motivation you have to do the things that you love. Individuals who are stressed often feel stagnated. Usually, you may have the feeling that things are not working out for you and this leaves you hopeless. Instead of taking action to change your life, you give up because nothing seems to work.

Visualization can turn this feeling around. Stress and anxiety fill your mind with destructive thoughts. Since your thoughts are involved here, your emotions stand to be affected, both in the short and in the long run. Visualization for self-motivation can help you regain control of your thoughts and turn the destructive thinking into positive thinking.

Ask yourself, what do you think successful people think about most of the time? Obviously, these people spend most of their time thinking about good things. They focus on what they want. That's the whole point of approaching life with optimism. You need to change your focus from thinking about what you don't want and thinking more about what you want.

So, as you use this visualization technique, know what you want and make it clear in your mind. For example, let's say you long to live in your dream home somewhere overseas, say in Australia.

Imagine yourself doing everything you can that will land you to your dream home. Reinforce your visualization by filling in all the fine details about your dream home in the location you've always wanted. Picture yourself settling down and making new friends with the locals. How do you feel about meeting new people? Imagine all the feelings that you will experience with your five senses.

It's through such visualization that you will push your mind to create ideas about how to make your dreams into a reality. At first, it may appear far-fetched. But visualization has nothing to do with knowing how you will get there. Picture yourself being in that moment and the universe will take its course.

The simplest trick behind visualization for self-motivation is to think about what you want. It's important that you develop a habit of visualizing every single day. Schedule it early in the morning and late at night moments before you go to bed.

Once the habit sticks and visualization is a non-negotiable part of your daily routine, you will find it easier to stay motivated throughout the day. The choices you make every day play a crucial part in determining how your life turns out. Therefore, if you build on your motivation to create a life that you desire every day, there is no doubt that your dreams will eventually come true.

The different visualization techniques discussed herein can be used for varying situations. Choose the best technique that suits your circumstance for the best results. For instance, when faced with a stressful situation, visualizing yourself in a happy memory can help distract your mind from negative emotions. If you're looking to get motivated as you seek to accomplish your goals, visualization for self-motivation will serve you best. The most important thing you should remember is to try your best to reinforce your visualization by adding all the little details about your mental picture. Include everything that touches on your five senses. Most importantly, visualize every single day.

Chapter 10: Combine All the Techniques in Your Daily Routine

At this point, you have learned how to practice several relaxation techniques. Maybe you've not mastered these techniques yet, but you're now aware of which techniques you should use for certain purposes. Based on experience, there are particular combinations of these relaxation strategies which creates maximum benefit to the user. This section will focus on the best blend to incorporate in your routine to reap maximum benefits from the relaxation techniques.

It's worth noting that combining two or more relaxation strategies provides you with a greater advantage simply because they create a synergistic effect. In other words, there is more to be gained by bringing together two or more techniques as compared to using one relaxation strategy alone.

Another convincing reason why you should consider combining relaxation techniques is that it helps to achieve a deepened state of relaxation as one technique builds on the calming effect of the other. Through the unique blend that we will recommend in this section, you will realize that each relaxation approach builds progressively on the preceding approach. Accordingly, there is a higher likelihood of achieving a deeper state of relaxation.

Besides, blending some of these techniques provides you with the unique benefit of saving time. You may be too busy to use one technique at a time; using two or more at a time can help you make use of the few minutes you have to perform a quick relaxation before proceeding with other important activities.

As you go through the different blends that we recommend, keep in mind that these are mere suggestions that have been proven and tested. You have the freedom to experiment with techniques that you think will serve you best. Of course, with constant practice, you will master these techniques and you will become more aware of which relaxation techniques that have a desired calming effect on you.

Fight-or-Flight Symptom Relief

The combinations presented below have been proven to be effective in relieving you of symptoms related to fight-or-flight response and stress-induced psychological issues.

Stretch and Relax

Sit comfortably on a chair and stretch your arms out. Now tighten your arms and pull them back to stretch your shoulders and chest. While doing that, tighten your legs by first curling your toes and then pulling them back to face you.

Place your right hand on your abdomen and take a deep breath in. As you breathe out, allow your hand to move with the flow of your air. Continue breathing in and out for about 10 seconds.

Gently close your eyes and start counting back from 10 to zero. Tell yourself that for every count you make, you will be more and more relaxed. Once you're through with the countdown repeat these phrases to yourself, "I am more and more peaceful and calm... I am getting more and more relaxed... I am drifting deeper and deeper into relaxation."

While in a calm state, visit your happy memory. Visualize a moment where you were totally happy and live in that moment for a few minutes. Ensure that you experience the feeling through all your senses.

When you feel that you've been in your happy memory long enough, start counting up from 1 to 10. Remind yourself that you're getting more and more alert as you finish the exercise.

I Am Grateful

There are times when you may feel like you started your day on the wrong foot. Usually, this happens when we notice that we're making mistakes in every step that we take. So, we panic and our anxiety levels go up. Our negativity bias gets the best of us and we begin feeling as though we are failures. Has this ever happened to you? You make one mistake and you feel like the world is crumbling down on you. When faced with such situations, consider using the following relaxation exercises.

Start by using the shorter version of the progressive muscle relaxation (PMR) technique we discussed in chapter 7. Curl your fists and flex your biceps. Smile widely as you wrinkle your forehead. Tense your back muscles and take a deep breath. Tense your feet by curling your toes and tightening the thighs, calves, and buttocks.

Now choose three things that have happened in your day so far that you feel grateful for. It doesn't matter whether it's a minor or major event. Choose anything that you're thankful for. It can be as simple as taking a hot shower in the morning or the breakfast that you enjoyed. It can be your colleague who helped you get to work on time or your child giving you a hug as you left for work in the morning. Take a moment or two to enjoy this experience as you relieve the stress that is slowly rising.

Continue savoring the moments that you're thankful for. Now take a first-person view of the things that you have done during the day that you are happy about. Remember, it doesn't have to be something major. Choose simple things that you did and they made your day feel worthwhile. For instance, maybe you finished a certain task on time or you helped your coworker manage something that was challenging. Stay in these positive experiences for a few minutes.

Deep Affirmation

Make yourself comfortable and take a few deep breaths in and out. While you're doing this, place your hand on your abdomen so you can notice your movements as you breathe in and out.

Gently close your eyes and perform a quick body scan from head to toe. Notice any tensions in your body. Progressively move from the top of your head as you determine whether there is any point in your body that feels tense. When you uncover a tense area, exaggerate it to raise your awareness. Tense the area where you feel some tightness, then pause for a second or two and release the tension.

Clear your mind as you strive to achieve a calm state of mind and body. Use your breathing as your object of focus to help relax your mind and clear clutter.

Now recite these affirmations with conviction.

I am happy and at peace.

Tension is draining out of my body.

I can tone down my level of tension at will.

I see peace within myself.

I am in touch with my inner peaceful self.

Relaxation is within my reach.

Note: You can edit these affirmations to suit a situation that you need to reaffirm to yourself. Maybe you're looking to make yourself feel happy or motivated. Adjust these affirmations to match that.

Once you feel relaxed long enough, stop and count from 1 to 10. Remind yourself that you're moving towards a more alert state.

Taking Control

Make yourself comfortable either on the floor or on a chair. Gently close your eyes and focus on your breathing. Notice each breath you take and the effect it has on your body. As you breathe out, imagine tension leaving your body like waves. Visualize these waves deeply. What color are these waves? Which part of your body is releasing the most waves?

Shift your attention to a situation that is making you feel stressed. Don't associate yourself with the stressful situation, just notice it. Now visualize feeling good that the situation has been resolved. Picture yourself feeling grateful that you managed to find a solution to the problem. Don't focus on the details, simply savor the good sensations flowing within you now that the problem is resolved. Remind yourself that you can handle any issue that you may be facing and be confident about it.

You can see how easy it is to combine two or more relaxation techniques. Challenge yourself to combine the techniques that work best for you. The more you practice these techniques, the better you get at it.

Set Your Goals and Manage Your Time Wisely

The relaxation techniques discussed in this manual are indeed effective and they have been proven and tested by people all over the world. Regardless of how effective these techniques are, if you fail to incorporate them into your busy daily schedule, you might not benefit from them. This is where the issue of time comes into play. Just like hitting the gym and exercising regularly, most people will argue that they don't have time to practice these relaxation approaches every day. But guess what, you have time. The only issue that you're facing is that you have poor time management. It's for this reason that I will briefly tip you on how you can include these exercises on your everyday routine without struggling.

Set Clear Goals

Successful people have one thing in common: they have clear goals. Setting clear goals helps you to prioritize activities. The idea of setting goals doesn't necessarily mean that you should set long term goals. You can have mini-goals that you plan to accomplish before the end of the day. These mini-goals can be in the form of a to-do list. Your to-do list will help you plan your day effectively. You will be better placed to attend to the most important activities first before proceeding to do other things.

If you can complete your tasks in time, you will have a lot of spare time for other activities such as spending time with your family and friends. The few minutes or hours you create can also be used to engage in self-care.

Effective Time Management

With regards to effective time management, the following time management techniques should help you.

Eat That Frog

Mark Twain once argued that if you can eat a live frog in the morning, then you would probably go through the day with the satisfaction that there nothing worse that can happen throughout the day. The term "frog" here is used to refer to your most important task. This is the one task that you might procrastinate (Tracy, 2019). Therefore, it is advisable that you accomplish this task early in the morning before doing anything else. This time management technique can help you prioritize the most important things that you need to do. For instance, focusing on yourself should be the first thing you do right after getting out of bed.

The Pomodoro Technique

This is another remarkable time management strategy that encourages you to use the time you have instead of working against it. The idea behind this technique is that you should break your daily schedule into 25-minute chunks (pomodoros) followed by five-minute breaks. Once you complete four pomodoros, you should take a longer break of approximately 15 - 20 minutes.

The main reason why this strategy is effective is that it instills a sense of urgency in you. Instead of assuming that you have the whole day to work on something, you will understand that you only have 25 minutes to make progress. This stops you from wasting your time on distractions. Ultimately, you're more likely to have time to practice relaxation techniques.

Say "No" and Delegate

Most people go through their days feeling like they have no time because they put a lot of pressure on themselves by taking on tasks they can't handle. It's time to stop this. We all have our limits. You cannot please everyone by taking on additional tasks in your already packed schedule. Learn to say "No." This is the best thing that you can do to help yourself have some extra time to focus on yourself and practice relaxation techniques.

You should realize that there is nothing wrong with admitting that you cannot handle certain tasks. Free yourself from pressure and delegate these tasks where possible.

Develop A Positive Addiction

It's possible to develop a "positive addiction" towards feeling good, confident and competent. This is something that you can practice regularly as it depends on the outlook that you have towards life. The positive addiction that you develop will encourage you to organize yourself in a way that you complete the most important activities first. With time, you will actually be addicted to the good feeling evoked when you accomplish these tasks. To achieve this, ensure that you set small, realistic goals that are attainable.

Final Thoughts

This guide has covered all you need to know about managing stress and anxiety through relaxation techniques. Ideally, by using these techniques regularly, you will be better placed to live a happy and fulfilling life. At this point, you may have realized that there are certain things that you have been taking for granted and yet they can help you overcome stress and anxiety. Your breathing, for example, the art of breathing in and out is in itself a remedy that can ease tension in your body, mind and soul. After reading this book, you should make a deliberate effort to breathe mindfully as this can help calm your mind and bring you back to the present moment. Unfortunately, there are instances where you may find yourself skipping these relaxation techniques. The fast-paced environment that we live in can stop you from focusing on yourself. There are many things that require your attention and you can't deny the fact that things might get challenging.

However, it's important to remind yourself of the main reason why you're practicing these relaxation exercises. For instance, you want to live a happy life where you approach each day with a renewed sense of optimism. Maybe you're looking for motivation to face your everyday challenges. Life as we know it is full of ups and downs. For that reason, you need something that can remind you of your purpose for existence. In reality, connecting with your inner self is the best way in which you can truly understand who you are and your purpose in this world. Through your inner understanding, you can begin looking at life from a different perspective. You will understand that true happiness doesn't come from the external world or the material things that you have. True happiness comes from within.

Tapping into the power of your inner self is only possible through the relaxation techniques that have been discussed in this manual. Perhaps stress has been weighing down on you and it has stopped you from enjoying life. Make this book your best friend and refer to it each time you need to practice any of the relaxation exercises. You have the power to transform your life into the kind of life that you've always dreamed of. The only thing that is standing between you and your goals is your mind.

Following the bitter and tough experiences that you may have had in life, your mind might have made you believe that you cannot make it or that you're a failure. Well, guess what? These are just plain thoughts. They cannot determine your future if you learn how to control these thoughts and respond differently to them. For instance, practicing breathing exercises can shift your attention from focusing on destructive thoughts that influence how you behave. Through guided breathing meditation, you can learn how to notice your thoughts and any signs of tension in your body. You can combine this with visualization to evoke positive emotions that have a profound impact on your emotional state. At the end of the day, you will respond well without necessarily allowing stress and anxiety to get the best of you.

Conclusively, confront your excuses. Some of the excuses that you will give yourself to avoid practicing these relaxation exercises regularly are the same excuses that might have driven you to the situation you are in today. Perhaps you're a victim of procrastination. Maybe you always think that the best time to relax is when you have completed all the important tasks in your schedule. This strategy doesn't work since you may end up procrastinating in case other issues pop up. Make good use of the time management techniques pointed out in this guide. Remember, if you can manage your time well, you will manage your life well.

Good luck!

References

Buddy, T. (2016, February 2). Drinking to relieve stress may actually compound the problem.https://www.verywellmind.com/the-link-between-stress-and-alcohol-67239

Campbell, M. (n.d.). Meaning, origin and history of the name Jing. https://www.behindthename.com/name/jing

Conway, J. (2018, May 1). Plant-based foods: Consumer diet reasons U.S. 2017 L statistic. https://www.statista.com/statistics/753935/plant-based-food-diet-reasons/

Cronkleton, E. (2019). 10 breathing exercises to try: For stress, training & lung capacity. https://www.healthline.com/health/breathing-exercise#lions-breath

Destructive thinking: The hidden cause of stress. (2019, October 1). https://www.conovercompany.com/destructive-thinking-the-hidden-cause-of-stress/

Ducharme, J. (2018, May 8). A lot of Americans are more anxious than they were last year, a new poll says. https://time.com/5269371/americans-anxiety-poll/

Eat That Frog: Brian Tracy explains the truth about frogs | Brian... (2019, August 13). https://www.briantracy.com/blog/time-management/the-truth-about-frogs/

Fletcher, J. (2019). 4-7-8 breathing: How it works, benefits, and uses. https://www.medicalnewstoday.com/articles/324417

Jáuregui-Lobera, I., & Montes-Martínez, M. (2020). Emotional eating and obesity. Psychosomatic Medicine [Working Title]. doi:10.5772/intechopen.91734

Palermo, E. (2015, March 10). What is Qigong? https://www.livescience.com/38192-qigong.html

Rama, S. (n.d.). The Real Meaning of Meditation. https://yogainternational.com/article/view/the-real-meaning-of-meditation

The Recovery Village. (2020, April 7). Stress statistics. https://www.therecoveryvillage.com/mental-health/stress/related/stress-statistics/#gref

Schimelpfening, N. (2015, November 23). Why some people are more prone to depression than others. https://www.verywellmind.com/why-are-some-people-more-prone-to-depression-1067622

Selva, J. (2018). Albert Ellis' ABC model in the cognitive behavioral therapy spotlight. https://positivepsychology.com/albert-ellis-abc-model-rebt-cbt/

Star, K. (2012, January 25). How to use relaxation techniques for help with anxiety disorders. https://www.verywellmind.com/popular-relaxation-techniques-2584192

Tai chi: A gentle way to fight stress. (2018, September 26). https://www.mayoclinic.org/healthy-lifestyle/stress-management/in-depth/tai-chi/art-20045184

Tarantola, C. (2018, January 20). The proven health benefits of yoga and meditation. https://www.pharmacytimes.com/contributor/christina-tarantola/2018/01/the-surprising-ways-a-mindfulness-practice-can-improve-your-quality-of-life

Tarantola, C. (2018, January 1). The proven health benefits of yoga and meditation. https://www.pharmacytimes.com/contributor/christina-tarantola/2018/01/the-surprising-ways-a-mindfulness-practice-can-improve-your-quality-of-life

What Is Qi Energy? (n.d.). https://www.qienergyexercises.com/what-is-qi-energy.htm

Printed in Great Britain
by Amazon

58352937R00149